Allegory and the Modern Southern Novel

Allegory and the Modern Southern Novel

Jan Whitt

Mercer University Press
Macon, Georgia

ISBN 0-86554-397-6

Allegory and the Modern Southern Novel
copyright © 1994
Mercer University Press, Macon GA 31207

The paper used in this publication meets the minimum requirements of
American National Standard for Information Sciences—Permanence of
Paper for Printed Library Materials, ANSI Z39.48-1984.

Library of Congress Cataloging-in-Publication Data

Whitt, Jan.
    Allegory and the modern southern novel / Jan Whitt.
    x + 149 pp.   6 x 9"   (15 x 23 cm.)
    Includes bibliographical references (10 pp.) and index.
    ISBN 0-86554-397-6 (alk. paper)
    1. American fiction—Southern States—History and criticism.
2. American fiction—20th century—History and criticism.
3. Christian fiction, American—History and criticism. 4. Fiction—
Religious aspects—Christianity. 5. Southern States in literature.
6. Christianity and literature. 7. Allegory. I. Title.
PS261.W54   1993
813.009'975—dc20   93-36368
                                                    CIP

Contents

For Charles and Wintry

Preface

Allegory and the Modern Southern Novel relies upon prior research in literature, religious studies, philosophy, American studies, and the history of ideas. Primary sources abound, but most secondary sources have skirted the topic that interests me. For example, Angus Fletcher (*Allegory*) has traced the history of parable and allegory without dealing with Southern literature; Paul de Man has dealt extensively with the nature of symbols and allegorical language without stretching his work to include the modern Southern novel. Sacvan Bercovitch has noted clearly and effectively the Puritan insistence on typology and has pulled the thread through American literature without singling out the art of the South. Even Ursula Brumm, who produces some of the most perceptive work dealing with Christ figures and the parable, has examined William Faulkner without stretching her gaze. I see this study not as a landmark in the field of literary or religious studies, for others have pioneered the territory with precision and insight. *Allegory and the Modern Southern Novel*, however, takes a step beyond their work. Particular points of interest include a support for several Southern novels often overlooked, for reflections on the life of Christ (both subtle and blatant) in numerous Southern works, and for the emblematic nature of the Southern text, character, and setting.

From the survey of history, *Allegory and the Modern Southern Novel* moves toward what I term the violence of allegory, beginning with the writings of Nathaniel Hawthorne (especially his short stories and *The Scarlet Letter*) and Herman Melville (with special attention to *Billy Budd* and *The Confidence-Man*). It also must be a defense of allegory, which has been disparaged as a too-blatant system of correspondences that reduce the mysterious and profound to the concrete and simplistic. Allegory, however, is not reductive but expansive. One writes allegory when one has learned the limits of realism in dealing with the metaphysical. An example, of course, lies in the parables of Christ, for when he sought to explain what was for him a very concrete kingdom of heaven, he told a story of a mustard seed. It also will become clear how the Southern allegorical novel is set apart from the American myth of innocence and success.

The novel to be considered initially is *The Heart Is a Lonely Hunter,* an allegory of our search for ourselves. Faith is no option for the secular world portrayed here; the fictional characters choose instead a flesh-and-blood hero to take the place of the prophet from Nazareth. The cries of the characters go unheard. *Wise Blood* follows, for in it a minor character tells Haze Motes in a "sour triumphant voice," "Jesus been a long time gone." Herein lies the message of Flannery O'Connor's fictional world. For one to understand *Wise Blood* and tolerate its theological inflexibility, one must account for O'Connor's own religious vision, clarify the fundamentalist Protestant spirit central to her work, and understand new directions for allegory.

The failed messiahs of *Go Down, Moses* and the flicker of a candle of hope in *Light in August* point out Faulkner's use of the Christianity he saw practiced in the Deep South. Faulkner, unlike O'Connor or Walker Percy (who are avowedly Roman Catholic in their vision), uses scripture only as a metaphorical source for his description of the South and its people. However, his allegorical techniques and his reliance on the life of Christ for symbols and contrast make Faulkner a logical choice. His characters long for a Moses who will lead the people from enslavement. Except for an occasional character such as Gail Hightower, who moves into self-awareness, most of Faulkner's characters (including Joe Christmas, Ike McCaslin, and Gavin Stevens) cannot deliver their world because they cannot understand themselves.

Allegory and the Modern Southern Novel seeks to define allegory without omitting its rich symbolic potential, and to indicate why the Southern writers would choose a view of humankind consistent with the literary vision of Hawthorne and Melville and inconsistent with the American myth of opulence and innocence. Here it will be necessary to mention the role Calvinism has played in the development of religion in America, for the seeds of fundamentalist doctrine in the modern South may be found in Puritan sermons and John Calvin's statements of creed. In a significant sense, Christianity (as it provides for the Fall of man and woman in the mythical Garden of Eden) has become an allegory for Southern history as Southerners continue to deal with a past shadowed by slavery and hypocrisy. The knowledge that O'Connor, Carson McCullers, and Faulkner possess of the Bible will be obvious in a discussion of their choices of imagery and theme. The metaphysical questions delineated earlier will find substance, if not answers, in the allegorical reading of *Wise Blood, The Heart Is a Lonely Hunter, Go Down, Moses,* and *Light in August.*

Acknowledgments

No book writes itself, and within every author whisper many voices. Those who have helped me to write *Allegory and the Modern Southern Novel* may be unaware of their contributions, making it all the more important to offer them my gratitude.

First, I must thank Professors Andy and Rachel Moore of the Department of English at Baylor University, who walked with me when I began my pilgrimage into the land of magnolias and soft Southern drawls. They gave me both a deep respect for Southern writers and the permission to live the life Robert Frost describes in "Two Tramps at Mud Time": "My object in living is to unite/My avocation and my vocation/As my two eyes make one in sight."

Second, I thank Robert D. Richardson, Jr., friend and scholar, who introduced me to allegory in a study of Herman Melville at the University of Denver. I also thank Eric Gould and Stuart James, professors of English at the University of Denver during my years there. The first shared with me his sense of the modern; the latter, his love for William Faulkner.

Third, I thank my colleagues and friends in the School of Journalism and Mass Communication at the University of Colorado at Boulder, especially Dean Willard D. Rowland, who encourages the study of the humanities in a sea of social scientists. To the Committee on University Scholarly Publications at the University of Colorado go hearty thanks for the funding that made the book possible.

Fourth, I must acknowledge Ed Bonahue and others at the *Southern Literary Journal,* who published "The Loneliest Hunter" (Spring 1992), a portion of my chapter on Carson McCullers.

Finally, I thank Michael, Charles, and Wintry for their many years of love and support. Theirs have been the sweetest voices of all.

Many of those to whom I am indebted are unnamed here. They talked with me for hours about the lives and work of Flannery O'Connor, Eudora Welty, Carson McCullers, Robert Penn Warren, William Faulkner, Alice Walker, Tennessee Williams, Walker Percy, and the rest. You know who you are.

Jan Whitt
October 1993

Introduction

As the young lover of music in Carson McCullers' *The Heart Is a Lonely Hunter*, Mick Kelly faces the "terrible hurt" of life by listening to a symphony on her radio. Turning it off, Mick tells the reader that she now "felt good," and she whispers the following to herself: "Lord forgiveth me, for I knoweth not what I do." This reference to Jesus' words from the cross—as ambiguous to the adolescent speaker as they are initially to the reader—precede McCullers' explanation of Mick's feelings: "Everybody in the past few years knew there wasn't any real God. When she thought of what she used to imagine was God she could only see Mister Singer with a long, white sheet around him. God was silent. . . . She said the words again. . . 'Lord forgiveth me, for I knoweth not what I do.' "[1]

The Southern novels that constitute this study reveal characters trapped as Mick is, aware of their human frailty, asking forgiveness for something they often are unable to define. Haze Motes (*Wise Blood*), John Singer (*The Heart Is a Lonely Hunter*), Ike McCaslin (*Go Down, Moses*), and Gail Hightower (*Light in August*) seek understanding in spite of their human limitations and the apparent absence of God. Through allegory, Flannery O'Connor, Carson McCullers, and William Faulkner create characters who are larger than life, for all four become symbols in a fictional representation of life.

Certainly the four novels mentioned above deal uncompromisingly with two metaphysical issues: humanity's search for (1) God and the meaning of existence and (2) an understanding of one's own nature. In an excerpt from *The Gay Science*, translated by Walter Kaufman, Friedrich Nietzsche describes a madman who "lit a lantern in the bright morning hours, ran to the market place, and cried incessantly, 'I seek God! I seek God!' " His discovery is no different from that of much modern literature, and the madman's conclusion is the message of Nietzsche's allegory:

---

[1]Carson McCullers, *The Heart Is a Lonely Hunter* (Boston: Houghton Mifflin Company, 1940) 101-102.

> Whither is God! . . . I shall tell you. *We have killed him*—you and
> I. Do we not hear anything yet of the noise of the grave-diggers
> who are burying God? Do we not smell anything yet of God's
> decomposition? Gods too decompose. God is dead. God remains
> dead. And we have killed him. How shall we, the murderers of all
> murderers, comfort ourselves? What was the holiest and most
> powerful of all that the world has yet owned has bled to death
> under our knives. Who will wipe this blood off us?[2]

Such metaphysical questions are not easily addressed by realism, and
the modern Southern novelist, like Nietzsche, often chooses allegory as a way
to endure the silence that follows the asking. The pursuit of the unanswerable
questions concerning God and the nature of humanity is enriched and
complicated by the use of allegory as a symbolic system.

Along with the search for meaning, the main characters of this study
also are obsessed with the question revealed in Psalm 8:4—"What is man that
thou art mindful of him? And the son of man, that thou visitest him?" The
psalmist's perplexed cry concerning the nature of humanity will assuredly
remain unanswered. If one asks a literature class for an assessment of our
hidden self, students often respond with titles: *The Heart of Darkness, Lord of
the Flies, Paradise Lost, Deliverance.* Through diverse works such as these we
then face ourselves as unaware of our capacity for evil, corruptible in nature,
fallen, and vulnerable in either civilized or primitive worlds. Proposing a
definitive response to the biblical query would be laughable, and one must
acknowledge the complexities of the issue early in the study. Southern
literature concerns itself ultimately and deeply with what lies at the heart of
humankind and does not flinch or turn aside from the darkness in the human
spirit. *Allegory and the Modern Southern Novel* focuses on allegory as the often
chosen mode of expression for the Southern writer dealing with our place in
an indecipherable world. It also defends allegory as an artistic seed that fell on
parched critical ground during the nineteenth century.

The textual analysis in this study of *The Heart Is a Lonely Hunter, Wise
Blood, Go Down, Moses,* and *Light in August,* as well as other works such as *A
Fable* (Faulkner), *All the King's Men* (Robert Penn Warren), and *To Kill a
Mockingbird* (Harper Lee), indicates that the literature of the modern South

---

[2]Friedrich Nietzsche, *The Gay Science,* in *Existentialism from Dostoevsky to Sartre*
(New York: New American Library, 1975) 126.

relies profoundly on Christian imagery and the Old Testament view of humankind and God. These Southern novels, therefore, bear examination in a modern world literature characterized by skepticism and suspicion of creeds and traditional faiths.

While the study obviously will concern American literature—more specifically the Southern Renascence—its scope is not limited to the Deep South or even the North American continent. Allegory, of course, was not originally an American literary genre, and while it has been indispensable for the American obsession with religion through the centuries, it remains a genre for writers such as Vladimir Nabokov, Franz Kafka, and others to master practically and illuminate critically. Certainly, Nabokov ("Signs and Symbols") and Kafka ("The Hunger Artist," *Metamorphosis*, and *The Trial*) do not tie allegory to the Christian mythos as Southern writers will be shown to do, but the parallels in the treatment of allegory become notable. What follows this section is a survey of allegory as it reached the South from New England sermons and fiction.

Characters in Southern novels often long for deliverance, for a savior. Certainly, we cannot ignore the title *Go Down, Moses* or call the selection of the names Jack Burden (*All the King's Men*) or Joanna Burden (*Light in August*) mere coincidence. Humanism, with its belief in our ability to redeem ourselves, and fundamentalist Christianity, with its focus on confession of sin as the means to salvation, continue at each other's throats in the contemporary South. Tent revivals and hymn lyrics—such as "Amazing grace, how sweet the sound/That saved a wretch like me"—attest to the fundamentalist's conclusion concerning human nature. While the Southern writers discussed in this study seem to long for belief in human perfectibility, they also conclude their search with a plea for a new messiah, a secular healer who might assuage the guilt that filters through history and consumes an entire region. Like Mick, their central characters seek forgiveness for possible sins committed in ignorance.

Often one learns that all one need fear is the unknown in one's own soul. Throughout American literature, one finds figures as disparate as John Winthrop and Roger Williams, Nathaniel Hawthorne and Ralph Waldo Emerson, Emily Dickinson and Henry David Thoreau, and Herman Melville and Walt Whitman. The gap between Winthrop and Williams concerning the capability of people to govern themselves and to strive for a democratic society is preserved in the allegories of Hawthorne (such as "The Minister's Black Veil," "Young Goodman Brown," "Ethan Brand," *The Scarlet Letter*) versus the essays of Emerson (especially "Self-Reliance" and "The Divinity School

Address"). The concern with death and judgment in the poems of Dickinson exists against the wholehearted assent given to nature, individualism, and beauty by Thoreau in *Walden*. The unsolvable moral dilemmas represented in Melville's *Moby-Dick*, *Billy Budd*, and *Benito Cereno* lie juxtaposed to the affirmation in Whitman's verse. Dividing these and other writers is their evaluation of the worth of the individual, their view of one's need for deliverance.

The South revealed by O'Connor, McCullers, and Faulkner has entered its own dark cave, has met itself, and has emerged after its exploration seeking a kind of literary absolution. Well aware that history cannot be rewritten, their South nonetheless seems to long for at least a fictional release from its collective guilt. Faulkner changes the title *Dark House* to *Light in August*, Haze Motes blinds himself in order to see in *Wise Blood*, and John Singer finds himself beset by unwanted disciples in *The Heart Is a Lonely Hunter*. Even in a predominantly realistic novel such as *All the King's Men*, Jack Burden determines to save himself from the intricate web of history and the mistakes of would-be savior Willie Stark. Also, the reenactment of the Fall in which Cass Mastern stumbles upon the cost of "sin" can be easily defined as allegory, and it is this incident taken from "history," of course, on which Burden's experiences and realizations pivot.

In the novels of O'Connor, McCullers, Faulkner, and others, one finds Southern messiahs—usually failed ones—who testify to the cultural longing for redemption. Theologian Paul Tillich points to a national loss of religious sensibility in his essay "The Lost Dimension in Religion," and his warnings have merit on many levels. Nonetheless, the South is hardly unaware of the need for religion as Tillich defines it, and it stands as the American region convinced on both secular and religious planes of the evil within humankind. As such, the South as a region becomes an effective metaphor for America. Admittedly, few if any summary statements concerning the South or its people are safe, but generalizations will be made for purposes of argument and in the spirit of a seminal text such as *The Mind of the South* by W. J. Cash.

America's dreams of individualism, material success, and moral superiority leave a bitter taste in a Southerner's mouth, for he or she has seen the ravages of internal war and the cost of sin. The slavery Southerners once supported even within the walls of their churches damns them. The South has known the loss of a generation of young men, the destruction of the land it prized even above family, and the weight of religious hypocrisy. While many claim that the region does not in reality share the religious fervor and self-abnegation of the Calvinist faith, the South nevertheless turns away with Hawthorne and Melville from the Transcendentalists and their soaring hopes for humanity. The doubt of the Southerner is as intensely internal as the doubt that surfaces in the sonnets of Gerard Manley Hopkins, who must face the contradictions of a faith he holds tightly. The God into whom the Southerner breathed life has turned his face away; one cannot deny the cries that follow his desertion of humankind.

The collective conscience of the South has not been redeemed via the fundamentalist faith to which it has clung, nor has ostracizing itself from the remainder of the nation lightened its burden or increased its regional pride. The South has fought two wars; the Civil War cost it its way of life and forced it, like Clytie of Eudora Welty's tale, to see its face honestly for the first time. Once upheld by the economic system and ignored by the church, slavery lurks like a phantom in the history of the region, and neither confession nor concession can clear a Southerner's view of his or her ancestors. The economy of the South has failed (Mississippi is still the poorest state in the nation); its educational institutions are not considered as prestigious as those of its Northern counterparts; and its practice of fundamentalist Christianity often oppresses women and blacks and suppresses the intellect.

Yet the South continues to fight a second war, often as ineffectively as it battled the advanced technology, superior artillery, and extensive railroads of the North. It still seeks to defend—not land or states' rights—but an agrarian, family-oriented mindset lauded in early books such as *I'll Take My Stand*. Nonetheless, just as the values of the South belong to others as well, so Southern literature is not a regional literature, any more than guilt, fear, displacement, and loss are peculiarly Southern preoccupations. It is in the realization of this fact that allegory is born, and a Southern landscape can begin to represent more than a specific scene in rural Georgia.

The story of the South is the story of a region that discovered that sin has nothing to do with serpents, and self-doubt has little to do with losing at Gettysburg. In this study, the Southern writer will be shown to acknowledge the dark side of the human soul and to determine to turn and confront the past. Through allegory, the South ceases to be a place in Macon, Mobile, or Baton Rouge. Being Southern becomes a way of seeing oneself. Because O'Connor, McCullers, and Faulkner have discovered what I call the heresy of self-reliance, the region they portray stands as the most effective metaphor for America; the South is a necessary reminder of the human longing for restitution and the desire for salvation. The Bible they offer is not Job, or Lamentations, or even Genesis, but the Southern novel.

Chapter 1

The Evolution of Allegory in America

1. Fallen Humanity and the Spark of the Divine

Christianity simply does not exist. If the human race had risen in rebellion against God and cast Christianity off from it or away from it, it would not have been nearly so dangerous as this knavishness of doing away with Christianity by a false way of spreading it.

> —Søren Kierkegaard
> *Fatherland* (1855)

It is but a shadow vanished, a bubble broke, a dream finished.

> —Roger Williams
> Letter to Major Mason (1670)

The brand of Christianity that the Puritans practiced and that Søren Kierkegaard rebuked has lost the connection between signifier and signified. To the Puritans, Christ was no longer the merciful savior of the New Testament but a rigid taskmaster; the cross no longer a symbol of divine love but an instrument of oppression and guilt; the world no longer the evidence of God's creative energy but a breeding place for evil. The excessively rigid religious system largely originated by John Calvin and exercised by the Puritans of New England provided spiritual security at the expense of personal freedom. (It was no wonder that the prison and the cemetery were two of the first areas to spring up in early Puritan settlements, since punishment and death were an intrinsic part of the political order.) It is also no wonder that writing about Puritan culture involves a study of dualisms and ambiguities, for at the root of Puritan religious life lie many ironies.

For example, the cross Christ died upon at once represented suffering and transfiguration. The belief that people are inherently evil found an unusual contradiction in the belief that God's own Son was sent to die for them. Reconciling law and passion, good and evil, order and chaos, and the law and personal revelation had been of central interest to the Puritan community; all revolve around the Puritan view of humankind as fallen. Yet while Puritan leaders often could not admit the necessity of both the law (or religion) and moral flexibility (or theological freedom), they had great faith in several human characteristics, especially the ability to learn. Perry Miller says, "That man was, however much deformed by sin and passion, essentially a rational and responsible being was just as much an axiom of their thought as that he needed to wait upon God for the special grace that would bring him to salvation."[1]

At the heart of the contradictions in early America, then, is the notion that people, though "deformed by sin and passion," as Miller writes, were also responsible and rational beings. The political and judicial systems established, however, undeniably cater to the former view. Puritan religion was most debilitating in its ignoring chance in human affairs and in its inability to reconcile dualities. While good and evil were poles apart to the Puritan community, John Milton had viewed them as inextricable and saw doubt and searching as inevitable evidences of faith. Untested Christianity was to Milton like a "fugitive and cloistered virtue" that "never sallies out and sees her adversary." In "Areopagitica," he writes, "To be still searching what we know not by what we know, still closing up truth to truth as we find it . . . this is the golden rule in theology as well as in arithmetic, and makes up the best harmony in a church; not the forced and outward union of cold and neutral and inwardly divided minds."[2] While people had minds made in the image of God's mind, they had to be guided. Also, as the chosen people of God, the Puritans could mete out law and punishment to fallen humanity as if by divine decree; their victims were regarded as having been struck by the hand of God himself. In *History of Plimoth Plantation*, William Bradford relates the end of a "proud and very profane yonge man" who cursed the Pilgrim travelers: "But

---

[1] *The Puritans,* ed. Perry Miller and Thomas H. Johnson, 2 vols. (New York: Harper and Row, 1963) 1:24.

[2] *The Norton Anthology of English Literature,* ed. M. H. Abrams, 2 vols. (New York: W. W. Norton and Co., 1968) 1:1027, 1032.

it pleased God before they came halfe seas over, to smite this yong man with a greveous disease, of which he dyed in a desperate maner. . . . Thus his curses light on his owne head; and it was an astonishment to all his fellows, for they noted it to be the just hand of God upon him."[3]

In the Puritans' focus on the Old Testament eye-for-an-eye justice, one sees again their inability to resolve contradictions. The new law established by Christ was characterized by mercy and humility. For example, in the story of the woman caught in adultery, the Bible relates, "So when they continued asking him, he lifted up himself, and said unto them, He that is without sin among you, let him first cast a stone at her" (John 8:7). The tunnel vision of the Puritans also overlooked much of Paul's doctrine: "Therefore, thou art inexcusable, O man, whosoever thou art that judgest: for wherein thou judgest another, thou condemnest thyself; for thou that judgest doest the same things" (Rom 2:1). In fact, *The Scarlet Letter* is a powerful fictional record asserting that inflexible laws and religions are an expensive way to guarantee order. While the novel is most certainly fiction and while the Puritan community has often been unfairly characterized, the stereotypical Puritan is not as caricatured as one might hope.

What one must not forget, however, is that the rigid systems were products of a single philosophy: a human being was wicked and had to be protected from himself or herself. John Wise writes in "Vindication of the Government of New-England Churches" (1717),

> For that the true and leading cause of forming Governments, and yielding up Natural Liberty, and throwing Man's equality into a Common Pile to be new cast by the Rules of fellowship, was really and truly to guard themselves against the Injuries men were lyable to Interchangeably; for none so Good to Man, as Man, and yet none a greater Enemy.[4]

In making a distinction between natural and divine liberty, John Winthrop writes in his "Speech to the General Court" (1645), "The exercise and maintaining of [natural] liberty makes men grow more evil, and in time to be worse than brute beasts."[5]

---

[3]Miller and Johnson, *The Puritans*, 1:98.
[4]Ibid., 1:264.
[5]Ibid., 1:206.

The disgust of the righteous before themselves and other sinners knew no bounds. In "Meditation 38," Edward Taylor queries, "Oh! What a thing is Man? Lord, who am I?"[6] In "Meditation 3," he cries, "Is't possible such glory, Lord, ere should/Center its Love on me Sins Dunghill else?"[7] Taylor chooses phrases such as "Leprosie of Sin" and "brissled sins," leaving no doubt of his perception of the human capacity for evil. However, it remains for Jonathan Edwards—more than fifty years later—to put humankind even more in the shadow of evil. In "Sinners in the Hands of an Angry God," Edwards tells his listeners, "There is laid in the very nature of carnal men, a foundation for the torments of hell; there are those corrupt principles, in reigning power in them, and in full possession of them, that are the beginnings of hell-fire."[8] While the latter-day Puritan's view makes a humanist shudder, it is Edwards' view of God that staggers many:

> The God that holds you over the pit of hell, much as one holds a spider, or some loathsome insect, over the fire, abhors you and is dreadfully provoked; His wrath towards you burns like fire; He looks upon you as worthy of nothing else but to be cast into the fire; He is of purer eyes than to bear to have you in His sight; you are ten thousand times more abominable in His eyes than the most hateful and venomous serpent is in ours.[9]

It surely is no wonder that Transcendentalism took root, for its views offered hope to a world weary with guilt and with a God who meted out grace randomly and without demonstrable compassion. The "vile wretches" "wallowing in all kind of sin"[10] in Michael Wigglesworth's *Day of Doom* had little hope apart from what Miller calls a "special infusion of grace"—and yet even this was apportioned according to God's "sovereign pleasure."[11]

The debate continues: How much of Puritanism was based on the doctrines of Calvin? Were there areas in which the Puritans softened the

---

[6]Ibid., 2:656i.

[7]Ibid., 2:656k.

[8]*Anthology of American Literature*, ed. George McMichael, 2d ed., 2 vols. (New York: Macmillan Publishing Co., 1980) 1:238.

[9]McMichael, *Anthology of American Literature*, 1:242.

[10]Ibid., 1:114.

[11]Miller and Johnson, *The Puritans*, 1:56.

demands Calvin made of his fellows, or areas in which Puritan leaders intensified his teachings and chained their followers even more tightly? While critics continue to disagree, it remains important to deal with the philosophical basis of Puritanism as a New England movement and to note at least where Calvinism and Puritanism cross and merge. Those such as Everett Emerson who seek to distinguish between the movements focus on minor points. In *Puritanism in America*, Emerson lists American Puritanism as giving a higher priority to preaching, as emphasizing more the process of salvation, and as being less concerned with what he calls "strictly theological issues."[12] Alden T. Vaughan and Francis J. Bremer, through the essays in *Puritan New England*, develop the thesis that Calvin was important to both Puritan and Anglican thinkers, although the latter emphasized Calvin less and less as time wore on. In this collection of essays, Ronald J. Vander Molen writes that as Puritans "grew more confident of their biblical scholarship, they shed all appeal to the authority of other scholars, Calvin included."[13] Calvinism, claims Miller, was being modified by 1630; the Puritans certainly did not take Calvin's system to America "inviolate": "The New England leaders did not stem directly from Calvin; they learned the Calvinist theology only after it had been improved, embellished, and in many respects transformed by a host of hard-thinking expounders and critics."[14] Richard L. Bushman comes the closest to a non-conclusive conclusive statement when he calls Calvinism the "structure of feeling" behind Puritanism.[15]

Feeling, however, had little to do with the "Five Points of Calvinism" authored at the Synod of Dort (1618) by Calvinists in order to refute new Arminian heresies. The points, as explained by David N. Steele and Curtis C. Thomas, include beliefs in: (1) Predestination (God elects on the basis of "foreseen belief"); (2) Limited atonement (Christ died for the world but only elected believers are saved); (3) Total depravity (people are so depraved that grace must precede faith and any good deed); (4) Irresistible grace (if God saves someone, the person cannot refuse Him); and (5) Perseverance of the saints (a

---

[12]Everett Emerson, *Puritanism in America* (Boston: Twayne Publishers, 1977) iii.

[13]Ronald J. Vander Molen, "Anglican Against Puritan," in *Puritan New England*, ed. Alden T. Vaughan and Francis J. Bremer (New York: St. Martin's Press, 1977) 10.

[14]Perry Miller, "The Marrow of Puritan Divinity," in *Puritan New England*, 44.

[15]Richard L. Bushman, "Jonathan Edwards and Puritan Consciousness," in *Puritan New England*, 347.

believer chosen by God cannot lose his or her salvation).[16] The dispute between the followers of Dutch Calvinist James Arminius and the Calvinists centered upon free will. Basically, the Arminians contended that divine grace may be resisted and believers may lose their salvation if they so choose. As Steele and Thomas state, the Calvinists wanted it clear that even faith itself was part of God's gift of salvation, not the "sinner's gift to God."[17] Humankind, then, had no role in coming to God: "Adam's fall had completely ruined the race," they write. "It was not man, but God, who determined which sinners would be shown mercy and saved."[18] While English Puritans were known primarily for practicing moral strictness and opposing the elaborate Mass and the complicated system of penance in the Roman Catholic and Anglican churches, many agree with the critic Emerson who says the Puritans were most clearly defined as Calvinists until after the rise of Cotton Mather (post-1730).

The Calvinist doctrines that amplify the five points stated earlier and that most profoundly affected the development of American Puritanism include (1) the mysteriousness of God the Father, (2) the problems that arise when an individual cannot know if God has elected him or her, (3) the plight of a degraded person called to do good, and (4) the supremacy of Scripture in governing the world. Calvin was a stern taskmaster, asking of others what he demanded of himself. As John Dillenberger, editor of a collection of Calvin's works, writes, "There is no evidence that poetry or art were media which stirred his sensibilities. Even his letters are like mannerist paintings, suffering a certain lack of warmth and compassion."[19] Calvin emphasized an all-powerful, all-knowing God, what Miller calls the "ultimate secret": "The English Puritans may be called Calvinists primarily because they held this central conception, though the thought is older in Christian history than Calvin, and they did not necessarily come to it under Calvin's own tuition."[20]

By 1630, Catholic, Lutheran, and Anglican critics of Calvinism were pointing out that predestination—for the one who believes oneself elected—can lead to self-righteousness. They also condemned Calvinism for not dealing

---

[16]David N. Steele and Curtis C. Thomas, *The Five Points of Calvinism* (Philadelphia: Presbyterian and Reformed Publishing Co., 1965) 13.

[17]Ibid., 16.

[18]Ibid., 18.

[19]John Dillenberger, *John Calvin: Selections from His Writings* (New York: Doubleday and Company, 1971) 11.

[20]Miller, *Puritan New England,* 45.

with the fears and questions of those who believe themselves unregenerate. Puritans then began to soften the doctrine of predestination, for, as Miller says, Winthrop did not practice pure Calvinism. He organized the Massachusetts settlement according to a "miniature edition of the divine covenant,"[21] Miller writes. The covenant was a new notion, for through the divine covenant humanity made a compact with God. This, of course, is a step beyond Calvinism, for humanity has been deemed worthy enough to enter into a contract with God. Miller adds, "God's predestination is of course absolute. He picks and chooses without regard to merit. But in the covenant He has consented to bestow His favor upon those who fulfill the conditions, and to guarantee to those who do so the assurance of their salvation."[22] Calvin would not have approved of increasing human pride at the expense of acknowledging God as the only active agent in redemption. Instead of understanding predestination as a threat to people, Calvin had considered it "consolation to the believer," claims Dillenberger: "[Calvin] found emancipation and joy in the fact that the world was securely in the hands of God and that the believer who had received the gift of faith could believe that God had destined him for the present and for the future."[23]

Thirdly, many began to have trouble reconciling the Calvinistic doctrine of a degraded, sinful man or woman whom God expected to save the world. Bushman, who uses the terms *Calvinism* and *Puritanism* interchangeably in his article on Jonathan Edwards, says Calvinism "compelled a man to abase and abhor himself totally": "Edwards was remembered chiefly for inhuman strictness and his debasement of human powers. Puritanism came to stand for dreary self-restraint and joyless piety."[24] In 1536, Calvin published *Institutes of the Christian Religion*, a volume that would influence France, the Netherlands, Germany, Scotland, England, Ireland, and America. In *Institutes* II.ii.1, Calvin writes, "Man, being taught that he has nothing good left in his possession, and being surrounded on every side with the most miserable necessity should, nevertheless, be instructed to aspire to the good of which he is destitute."[25] What Calvin failed to understand, according to Miller, is that

---

[21]Ibid., 59.

[22]Ibid., 55.

[23]Dillenberger, *John Calvin: Selections*, 17.

[24]Bushman, "Jonathan Edwards and Puritan Consciousness," *Puritan New England*, 354, 360.

[25]Quoted by Perry Miller, in *Puritan New England*, 46.

deeds are not "merely the concomitants of faith, but can even be in themselves the beginning of faith."[26] And what Calvin further failed to see, it seems, is that those who believe themselves capable of good works are more likely to perform them.

Finally, Scripture became the absolute guide in matters of morality. Dillenberger, however, claims that for Calvin, Scripture did not focus as much on the fundamentalist's notion of the inerrant Word of God as on the "conjunction of word and spirit."[27] No matter how one chooses to view the function of the Bible in the lives of the Puritans, the fact remains that a staggering gap existed between the New Testament portrait of God and the practices of his chosen people.

As Darrett Rutman asserts in *American Puritanism,* the center of Puritan theology was the Adamic legend; the ultimate purpose was regaining the Garden.[28] The Puritans had indeed, as Michael McGiffert terms it, "cracked their heads on Calvin."[29] It is Miller's article on "The Puritan State and Puritan Society" that best explains the system of government that evolved in Massachusetts. His thesis, simply, is that the "government of Massachusetts, and of Connecticut as well, was a dictatorship, not of a single tyrant, or of an economic class, or of a political faction, but of the holy and regenerate."[30] Society became an organism, established on the single truth the Puritans had failed to enforce in England. When more than 20,000 came to America, the Puritans crusaded anew against those with opposing views, and with more success. A brief list of forms of coercion the Puritans used follows:

> 1635—Roger Williams was banished from Massachusetts and founded the first Baptist church in 1639. (In 1654, Harvard president Henry Dunster became a Baptist and resigned; finally in 1681, the Massachusetts General Court voted to allow Boston Baptists to worship.)

---

[26]Ibid., 58.

[27]Dillenberger, *John Calvin: Selections,* 13.

[28]Darrett Rutman, *American Puritanism* (New York: J. B. Lippincott Company, 1970) 10.

[29]Michael McGiffert, *Puritanism and the American Experience* (Reading MS: Addison-Wesley, 1969) iv.

[30]Perry Miller, "The Puritan State and Puritan Society," in ibid., 43.

1637—Anne Hutchinson was banished from Massachusetts for her Antinomian beliefs.

1638—John Wheelwright, an Antinomian who supported Anne Hutchinson, was banished from Massachusetts.

1651—Three Baptists were fined and banished from Massachusetts.

1656—The first Quakers were arrested and banished from Massachusetts.

1658—The death penalty was invoked for Quakers who returned to Massachusetts following banishment.

1659—William Robinson and Marmaduke Stevenson, Quakers, were hanged in Boston.

1660—Mary Dyer, a Quaker and former Antinomian, was hanged in Boston.

1692—The cries of witchcraft, which were first raised in Connecticut in 1647, occurred again in Salem. More than 160 persons were accused during this year. The accusations did not die down for the remainder of the century until nearly 100 charges had been made and 38 persons had been executed.[31]

It took the action of Charles II in 1661 to bring the executions of Quakers to a close, and, according to Miller, "puzzlement" existed until the end of the seventeenth century among Puritan leaders of New England: "They could hardly understand what was happening in the world, and they could not for a long time be persuaded that they had any reason to be ashamed of their record of so many Quakers whipped, blasphemers punished by the amputation of ears, Antinomians exiled, Anabaptists fined, or witches executed."[32]

---

[31]Facts on witchcraft cited by John Demos, "Underlying Themes in the Witchcraft of Seventeenth-Century New England," *Puritan New England*, 253.

[32]Miller, *Puritanism and the American Experience*, 44.

On the flip side, of course, stand critics such as John T. McNeill, author of *The History and Character of Calvinism*, who—while he attests that Plymouth and Boston colonists were "definitely Calvinist"—dedicates his book as a sympathetic treatise to his father, "an exemplar of Calvinist faith and virtue."[33] He writes, "From John Cotton to Jonathan Edwards, New England Puritanism passed through an epoch of greatness and produced a type of human being that no just and informed mind can think of without admiration."[34] In spite of such a desire to rewrite history, the mutilation and death that came to men and women with ideas contrary to those of the Puritans is no fictional record.

Nathaniel Hawthorne and Herman Melville, as Kenneth Murdock has pointed out, took the Puritan theology—emphasis on sin, the struggle involved in spiritual development, and the ideal expressed in images and symbols—and transformed it into fiction. As early as 1657, twenty-one years before *Pilgrim's Progress*, an allegory emerged in London that was reprinted in Boston from 1683 to 1763. Called "A Rich Treasure At an easy Rate: or, The ready Way to true Content," the allegory shows the demise of Poverty and Sloth and Pride and Riches who live together, and the fruits of the companionship between Godliness and Labour. Allegory became a logical bridge between Puritan theology and New England fiction.

The implications of a world peopled with fallible, suffering human beings and governed by an arbitrary God influenced writers such as Melville, Hawthorne, and Emily Dickinson. A world in which elements in the physical world were reflections of the spiritual realm—where human actions sparked divine punishment—paved the way for allegory and its system of correspondences. As Robert E. Long points out, Hawthorne and Melville, too, regarded the physical world as a "symbolic chart containing concealed meanings"[35] relevant to each individual. This world view also set up the theological dilemmas that were to haunt American writers for centuries. Melville was—as T. Walter Herbert, Jr., writes—forced to explore the implications of Calvin's belief that "man cannot suffer unmerited affliction": "Like others who sought to conceive a God who respects the liberal estimate of man's dignity, Melville

---

[33]John T. McNeill, *The History and Character of Calvinism* (New York: Oxford University Press, 1954) dedication page.

[34]McNeill, *History and Character of Calvinism*, 340-41.

[35]Robert E. Long, *The Great Succession: Henry James and the Legacy of Hawthorne* (Pittsburgh: University of Pittsburgh Press, 1979) 4.

was forced to recognize that the spectacle of worldly evil created an anomaly, a body of undeniable fact that could not be digested within any scheme of supernal benevolence."[36] However, before one can explore the direct effects of Puritan doctrine on New England or Southern writers, one must examine the reaction of the Transcendentalists, for their reaction was a desperate cry for a belief in the dignity of the human being.

In many ways the Transcendentalist accomplishment was largely a radical shift in focus. Instead of asserting once again the Old Testament God of wrath, justice, and retribution, Ralph Waldo Emerson pointed toward the New Testament Gospels with their record of Christ as merciful friend. This role was often divorced from Christ's function as redeemer or savior, for if a person could save himself or herself via emulation of a Christ-like figure, where lay the need for a cross? Ursula Brumm writes that the Transcendentalists moved beyond the Unitarian theologian and made the Son of God a "figure of supreme humanity, whose brotherhood with man attests to man's divine nature."[37] Transcendentalism also concerned itself, as Brumm notes, with the divinity of Christ as well as the significance of miracles and the eternal. In "Divinity School Address," Emerson says of Jesus,

> He saw with open eye the mystery of the soul. Drawn by its severe harmony, ravished with its beauty, he lived in it, and had his being there. Alone in all history he estimated the greatness of man. One man was true to what is in you and me. He saw that God incarnates himself in man, and evermore goes forth anew to take possession of his world.[38]

It is this view of Christ as Supreme Man that challenged Emerson and led Theodore Parker to discount the dominant Christian perception of Christ as divine and the Bible as literal. For if Christ were truly the unique Son of God, Parker asked, where is the wonder, the miracle, in his life? "His virtue has no merit, his love no feeling, his cross no burden, his agony no pain. His death

---

[36]T. Walter Herbert, Jr., *Moby-Dick and Calvinism: A World Dismantled* (New Brunswick NJ: Rutgers University Press, 1977) 109.

[37]Ursula Brumm, *American Thought and Religious Typology* (New Brunswick NJ: Rutgers University Press, 1970) 203.

[38]*Ralph Waldo Emerson: Selected Prose and Poetry*, 2d ed. (New York: Holt, Rinehart, and Winston, Inc., 1969) 60.

is an illusion, his resurrection but a show. For if he were not a man, but a god, what are all these things? . . . Then his resignation is no lesson, his life no model, his death no triumph to you or me, who are not gods, but mortal men."[39] If humankind could aspire to stand as moral and intellectual equals with Christ, herein lay their greatness and hope. It was the assumption that people could indeed supersede rank humanity that led Henry David Thoreau to write in "Civil Disobedience," "I was not born to be forced. I will breathe after my own fashion."[40] A man or woman, thus, became the center of the universe and could dream dreams and chart a clear course through the world. Thoreau writes in *Walden*:

> I learned this, at least, by my experiment; that if one advances confidently in the direction of his dreams, and endeavors to live the life which he has imagined, he will meet with success unexpected in common hours. He will put some things behind, will pass an invisible boundary; new, universal, and more liberal laws will begin to establish themselves around and within him; or the old laws be expanded, and interpreted in his favor in a more liberal sense, and he will live with the license of a higher order of things.[41]

Individualism—separation from the world in an attempt to become our own best selves—lay at the base of Thoreau's Walden Pond experience. "Not till we are lost, in other words, not till we have lost the world, do we begin to find ourselves,"[42] he writes, echoing Scripture as Robert Frost was later to echo him in "Directive" ("And if you're lost enough to find yourself/By now").[43] This then translated itself into political theory, expressed in "Civil Disobedience": "There will never be a really free and enlightened State until the State comes to recognize the individual as a higher and independent power, from which all its own power and authority are derived, and treats him accordingly."[44]

---

[39]Quoted by Robert D. Richardson, Jr., *Myth and Literature in the American Renaissance* (Bloomington: Indiana University Press, 1978) 47.

[40] *The Portable Thoreau*, ed. Carl Bode (New York: Viking Press, 1947) 127.

[41]Ibid., 562.

[42]Ibid., 420.

[43] *The Poetry of Robert Frost*, ed. Edward C. Lathem (New York: Holt, Rinehart and Winston, 1969) 378.

[44] *The Portable Thoreau*, 136.

"Self-Reliance" (1841), one of the most dependable texts of Trans-cendental doctrine, shares many of the conclusions concerning human nature found in *Walden*. "A political victory, a rise of rents, the recovery of our sick, or the return of your absent friend, or some other favorable event raises your spirits, and you think good days are preparing for you," writes Emerson. Advocating the role of men and women as captains of their own fates, Emerson adds, "Do not believe it. Nothing can bring you peace but yourself."[45] Men and women will only know the range of power they possess over destiny, over their own spirits, when they learn what Jesus knew: how deeply worthy they are. "Thus is he," writes Emerson of Christ in the "Divinity School Address," the "only soul in history who has appreciated the worth of man."[46] Until he learns this, each man will be a "god in ruins," a "dwarf of himself."[47] The Transcendentalist's byword was "Trust thyself: every heart vibrates to that iron string" and "Insist on Yourself; never imitate."[48] If a person is indeed "part or parcel of God," if "the currents of the Universal Being circulate through me,"[49] then human beings are prisoners only to their perceptions of themselves. This belief produced great hope and determination; guilt, damnation, retribution, and fate were thrust into a dark closet of the past. Both Thomas Carlyle's *Heroes and Hero-Worship* and Emerson's "Self-Reliance" focused on history as the "biography of a few stout and earnest persons."[50] No longer the pawns of a vengeful, or at best mysterious creator, men and women could assert themselves as Christ had done and alter the course of their worlds. Evil became merely an absence of good; helplessness and despair, merely the responses of a lazy spirit. "Good is positive. Evil is merely privative, not absolute," writes Emerson. "It is like cold, which is the privation of heat."[51]

These were words of promise, of assurance. But the Puritan observation of humanity in turmoil, trapped within limitations and sin, was simply hidden away as the American spirit of democracy and pride flared. Lurking in the shadows was the fear that humankind might falter. The debate, of course, was not a new one; it would span the years from Scripture to

---

[45] *Ralph Waldo Emerson*, 93.
[46] Ibid., 61.
[47] *Nature*, in *Ralph Waldo Emerson*, 35.
[48] "Self-Reliance," in *Ralph Waldo Emerson*, 72, 90.
[49] *Nature*, in *Ralph Waldo Emerson*, 6.
[50] *Ralph Waldo Emerson*, 80.
[51] "The Divinity School Address," in *Ralph Waldo Emerson*, 58.

modern literature. Centuries before, Shakespeare had created a prince of
Denmark, who was in his own eyes a "rogue and peasant slave," a "dull and
muddy-mettled rascal."[52] Hamlet asks his heart's question to the air:

> What is a man,
> If his chief good and market of his time
> Be but to sleep and feed? A beast, no more.
> Sure he that made us with such large discourse,
> Looking before and after, gave us not
> That capability and godlike reason
> To fust in us unused.[53]

Because men and women are aware of the past and are both tormented and
blessed by an ability to mold their own futures, they are both animal and
angel, human and divine. Then, modernist Rainer Maria Rilke writes in his
"Eighth Elegy,"—"how confused is anything that comes/from a womb and has
to fly," how limited is humanity:

> All other creatures look into the Open
> With their whole eyes. But our eyes,
> turned inward, are set all around it like snares,
> trapping its way out to freedom.
> We know what's out there only from the animal's
> face; for we take even the youngest child,
> turn him around and force him to look
> at the past as formation, not that openness
> so deep within an animal's face. . . .
> Not for a single day, no, never have we had
> that pure space ahead of us, in which
> flowers endlessly open.[54]

Can we create our own destiny? Can a man or woman remake his or
her world? Or are we always inches away from a maelstrom of the past and of

---

[52]*Hamlet*, in *William Shakespeare: The Complete Works*, ed. Alfred Harbage
(Baltimore: Penguin Books, 1969) act 2, sc. 2, line 534; act 2, sc. 2, line 553.

[53]*Hamlet*, act 4, sc. 4, lines 33-39.

[54]Rainer Maria Rilke, *Duino Elegies and the Sonnets to Orpheus*, trans. A. Poulin, Jr.
(Boston: Houghton Mifflin, 1977) 59, 55.

human limitation? Is a man or woman responsible for the cruelty of others, for the emptiness and horror within his or her own soul? Both the Puritans and the Transcendentalists state their cases with conviction, and Hawthorne, Melville, and others will follow suit. The reply to Winthrop and Emerson did not, could not, take the form of realism. To contain the wrenching tensions of belief and disbelief in a compassionate-hostile/concerned-detached God, American writers turned back to the Bible for imagery and to allegory for form.

2. The Violence of Allegory in Hawthorne and Melville

Upon my honor, I am not quite sure that I entirely comprehend my own meaning in some of those blasted allegories.

—Nathaniel Hawthorne
Letter (1854)

Appreciation! Recognition! Is love appreciated? Why, ever since Adam, who has got to the meaning of this great allegory—the world? Then we pygmies must be content to have our paper allegories but ill comprehended.

—Herman Melville
Letter (1851)

All these things spake Jesus unto the multitude in parables; and without a parable spake he not unto them: That it might be fulfilled which was spoken by the prophet, saying, I will open my mouth in parables; I will utter things which have been kept secret from the foundation of the world.

—Matthew 13:34-35

Allegory has been disparaged as a too-blatant system of correspondences that reduces the mysterious and profound to the concrete and simplistic. By surveying the origin of allegory in American literature, one soon discovers that allegory is not reductive but expansive. When a writer such as Franz Kafka or Jorge Luis Borges either changes men into insects or sets up hopelessly forking paths, he has stepped onto a plane that defies realism—has tapped into what the Transcendentalists knew as the unified world of Spirit behind the "thing." When one creates allegory—whether as a writer or reader—one moves into the realm of faith. Allegory does not provide tidy systems, although we may speak of an "allegorical system"; rather, it is the product of oppositions and tensions one must somehow hold in balance. By understanding this, one begins to confront the violence or conflict inherent in allegory.

Literary scholars usually agree that allegory is extended metaphor; that it equates persons and actions with meanings that lie outside the text; that characters often are personifications; that events and settings may be historical or fictitious. What many critics have failed to emphasize, however, is that allegory operates as much through tension and concealment as through equations and correspondences. Christ's parables, woven with the threads of common occurrences and ordinary people, also stand on mystery. As Günther Bornkamm notes in *Jesus of Nazareth*, we are asked to grasp the infinite in tales of the everyday—to find God's kingdom in contradictions. Bornkamm writes,

> An unknown rabbi of Nazareth in a remote corner of Palestine? A handful of disciples, who, when it came to the showdown, left him in the lurch? A doubtful mob following him—publicans, loose women, sinners, and a few women and children and folk who got help from him? On his cross the sport of passersby? Is this the Kingdom of God?[55]

One must find the kingdom within a world that offers no sign of it, and the juxtaposition of visions is a violent one.

Yet one must not necessarily read for the moral or message within allegory—or even parable—for allegory points primarily to itself. As one examiner of metaphor and theology asserts, "It is not that the parable points to the unfamiliar but that it includes the unfamiliar within its boundaries."[56] The unfamiliar—the Mystery—therefore becomes the context for understanding ordinary human events. In the same way that the parable of the prodigal son may be read as a revelation of God's forgiveness, Jesus is himself a metaphor of God—here, the "transcendent comes to ordinary reality and disrupts it,"[57] writes Sallie TeSelle. Perception may well follow the cataclysmic appearance of Christ, but one has no choice but to deal with the violence of the encounter. The violence lies, as O'Connor reveals in *Wise Blood*, in the

[55]Günther Bornkamm, *Jesus of Nazareth* (New York: Harper and Row, 1960) 72-73.

[56]Sallie TeSelle, *Speaking in Parables: A Study in Metaphor and Theology* (Philadelphia: Fortress Press, 1975) 5-6.

[57]Ibid., 3.

explosion that occurs when the holy meets the unholy, when the transcendent meets the real.

Such violence is often a matter of equation, of interpretation. For example, in the parable of the prodigal, we are not confronted with a disparity of worlds. As TeSelle emphasizes, our concern is not how evident is the personality of God in the response of the father, but how "radical" love, faith, and hope are in the human world. Kafka's works are violent in still another way. His novels—perhaps the extreme allegorical event—are about the unfamiliar, the incomprehensible. They do not merely describe the incomprehensible, however, for the events the characters face do not, in fact, have meaning. When one looks in *The Trial* for the meaning of the quest, one meets the Void. Joseph K. and the reader are one, for the reader's world, too, is a fictional one, created as he or she lives it.

Allegory builds upon contradiction and surprising reversals; through its employment of symbols, its significance approaches that of myth. William Faulkner explains the appeal of his symbolic network by equating symbol with what is "instinct in man," what is available "in his inheritance of his old dreams, in his blood, perhaps his bones, rather than in the storehouse of his memory, his intellect."[58] As Thomas Carlyle and C. S. Lewis have noted, there is both revelation and concealment in symbol. While we shall fully examine this paradox in chapter 2, we must here acknowledge the contribution of symbol to the richness of allegory. As Arlin Turner says in his book on Nathaniel Hawthorne, allegory and symbolism have been artificially divided, and there is, he adds, no such distinction in Hawthorne's work:

> In recent usage, allegory and symbolism have been distinguished with some strictness, the first being taken to designate an equating, in a coldly mathematical way, of some quality with an appropriate object, or person, or act, and the second to indicate a more dramatic and a more richly suggestive relationship between an image and the meaning it suggests.[59]

As we shall find, allegory uses symbols, not to equate the thing with the idea, but to save itself from blatant personifications and rabid moralisms. The

---

[58]Quoted by James B. Meriwether and Michael Millgate, in *Lion in the Garden: Interviews with William Faulkner* (New York: Random House, 1968) 126.

[59]Arlin Turner, *Nathaniel Hawthorne* (New York: Barnes and Noble, 1961) 122-24.

tendency of writers like Melville and Hawthorne is, in fact, toward emblem, fable, and allegory. "Their characters," writes Robert E. Long, "are not free to belong wholly to the world; they are idealized, in the sense that they belong largely to the realm of moral abstraction."[60]

Neither the Puritans nor the Transcendentalists were, of course, unfamiliar with allegory. As students of the Bible, Puritans often dealt with symbols, typology, and parable. In fact, while often attacked for their plain style, the Puritans are defended by Sacvan Bercovitch, who notes that their writing was "highly figurative, abounding in metaphor, parallel, allusion, type and trope, and controlled by a variety of sophisticated rhetorical devices." He adds, "Their belief in 'spiritual signification' opened out into a richly symbolic mode of discourse."[61] Parables of Christ told the truth but told it slant, and Puritan theologians seemed to realize that God's kingdom often came in concealment. Their task was to decipher the evidence given in Scripture and in the natural world, and they took to the challenge with vigor. As John R. May notes, the parable achieves its effect "indirectly."[62] "A New Testament parable is a 'linguistic incarnation,' " agrees TeSelle, "and, like its teller, who himself was the parable of God, works by indirection."[63] While not as extended a metaphor as an allegory, parables do, TeSelle writes, "embrace the transcendent within the economic, vivid, immediate stories of human, very human beings."[64] In all parables—from Christ's tales of the good Samaritan and the lost sheep to Plato's cave to Bunyan's pilgrim to Kafka's alienated man—lies a mystery couched within the events of what Bornkamm calls the "familiar world, a comprehensible world, with all that goes on in the life of nature and of man, with all the manifold aspects of his experience, his acts and his sufferings."[65] To the Puritans, parables were evidence of a reality outside themselves, of a world beyond. TeSelle writes,

---

[60]Robert E. Long, *The Great Succession: Henry James and the Legacy of Hawthorne* (Pittsburgh: University of Pittsburgh Press, 1979) 4.

[61] *The American Puritan Imagination,* ed. Sacvan Bercovitch (New York: Cambridge University Press, 1974) 4-5.

[62]John R. May, *The Pruning Word: The Parables of Flannery O'Connor* (Notre Dame: University of Notre Dame Press, 1976) 14.

[63]TeSelle, *Speaking in Parables*, 71.

[64]Ibid., 37.

[65]Bornkamm, *Jesus of Nazareth*, 69.

The unfamiliar (the kingdom of God) is the context, the interpretative framework, for understanding life in this world. We are not taken out of this world when we enter the world of the parable, but we find ourselves in a world that is itself two-dimensional, a world in which the "religious" dimension comes to the "secular" and reforms it.[66]

Finding the supernatural in the familiar was, as we have seen, a common practice for Emerson and Thoreau as well. Just as Erich Auerbach states in *Scenes from the Drama of European Literature,* "One cannot address the 'supernatural order' as such, one can only address its incarnate revelation."[67] Angus Fletcher is correct when he says that Christianity has made the art of allegory easier because it sees creation as an "establishment of a universal symbolic vocabulary."[68] It is this fact, of course, that links Emerson undeniably to the Puritans and gives meaning to his statement that "good writing and brilliant discourse are perpetual allegories."[69] Natural facts point one toward spiritual truths, Emerson believed, but Mason Lowance, Jr., notes that long before Emerson, Jonathan Edwards was familiar with the Platonic conception of a "spiritual universe that lies beyond the physical world, which is its representation or symbol only."[70]

Allegory is born when one recognizes the limits of realism. When writers have set out on a metaphysical quest, when their meaning lies beyond the familiar, common, recognizable patterns of reality, they move into allegory. If a Southerner were to write a realistic chronicle of the post-Civil War South, it would be a limited regional account with universal significance only in its portrayal of character. But when Faulkner creates a Gail Hightower who stands at a darkened window and wrestles with the past, when O'Connor writes of Haze Motes who blinds himself physically in order to see spiritually, the South

---

[66]TeSelle, *Speaking in Parables,* 6.

[67]Erich Auerbach, *Scenes from the Drama of European Literature* (New York: Meridian Books, 1959) 75.

[68]Angus Fletcher, *Allegory: The Theory of a Symbolic Mode* (Ithaca NY: Cornell University Press, 1964) 130.

[69]*Nature,* in *Ralph Waldo Emerson,* 15.

[70]Mason Lowance, Jr., "Images or Shadows of Divine Things in the Thought of Jonathan Edwards," in *Typology and Early American Literature,* ed. Sacvan Bercovitch (Amherst: University of Massachusetts Press, 1972) 210.

as a region becomes irrelevant. Paul de Man helps clarify what has been accomplished by Melville, Hawthorne, T.S. Eliot, and the Southern writers to be dealt with in this study. In his comments, one discovers the transcendent potential of allegory: "Whereas the schizophrenic often evades his double-bind by creating verbal fantasies, the persistent impulse of allegory is to evade cultural psychosis by creating a 'higher' sense in which the original text can be taken— that is, a sense clearly not inherent in the signifying system of the text itself."[71] As Fletcher notes, allegories are not "dull systems" but "symbolic power struggles."[72] This is complicated by the fact that allegories point both toward and away from themselves; they often point outside plot and character to a higher truth. This is possible, de Man would argue, because allegories are born in a desperate attempt to capture in earthly terms what lies in the spiritual realm. The allegorist may find himself crying, like Benjy in *The Sound and the Fury*, "I tried to say, but they went on, and I went along the fence, trying to say. . . ."[73]

Although Hawthorne chose allegory as the only appropriate avenue for his message, he nonetheless doubted its effectiveness. He was, however, consistent in his portrayal of humankind. The dark heart of humanity lies at the center of most of his tales, including "Young Goodman Brown," "The Minister's Black Veil," "Ethan Brand," "Roger Malvin's Burial," and even his novel *The Scarlet Letter*. Reuben Bourne, who had promised his wife Dorcas to look after her father during the war, leaves the older man before he dies, promising to go for help. He never returns, and in "Roger Malvin's Burial," Hawthorne uncovers Reuben's hidden sin by revealing, "But year after year that summons, unheard but felt, was disobeyed. His one secret thought became like a chain binding down his spirit like a serpent gnawing into his heart; and he was transformed into a sad and downcast yet irritable man."[74] When the minister preaches in "The Minister's Black Veil," the narrator tells us, "The subject had reference to secret sin, and those sad mysteries which we hide from our nearest and dearest, and would fain conceal from our own

---

[71]Paul de Man, *Allegories of Reading: Figural Language in Rousseau, Nietzsche, Rilke, and Proust* (New Haven: Yale University Press, 1979) 12.
[72]Fletcher, *Allegory*, 23.
[73]William Faulkner, *The Sound and the Fury* (New York: Random House, 1929) 63.
[74]*Great Short Works of Hawthorne*, ed. Frederick C. Crews (New York: Harper and Row, 1967) 261.

consciousness."[75] In "Young Goodman Brown," Satan introduces Brown to what Hawthorne calls the "deep mystery of sin." Earth, we are told, is "one stain of guilt, one mighty blood spot." "Evil is the nature of mankind," Satan says in the dark shadows during the forest scene. "Evil must be your only happiness. Welcome again, my children, to the communion of your race."[76]

As in *The Scarlet Letter* when Arthur Dimmesdale is tempted to trap the innocents in his congregation, Brown feels a "loathful brotherhood" with his townspeople "by the sympathy of all that was wicked in his heart."[77] The guilt of hidden sin is nowhere more powerfully conveyed than in "The Minister's Black Veil," in which Hawthorne writes, "Each member of the congregation, the most innocent girl, and the man of hardened breast, felt as if the preacher had crept upon them, behind his awful veil, and discovered their hoarded iniquity of deed or thought."[78] The only escape from guilt and despair is suffering and self-denial. In *The Scarlet Letter*, Hester loses Dimmesdale and lives out her life alone in a forest cottage. In "Roger Malvin's Burial," the resolution and divine retribution are even more dramatic. While hunting, Bourne accidentally shoots his son, Cyrus. An allegorical mirror of Abraham and Isaac and God and Christ, the tale ends with Bourne finding peace through loss:

> Then Reuben's heart was stricken, and the tears gushed out like water from a rock. The vow that the wounded youth had made the blighted man had come to redeem. His sin was expiated—the curse was gone from him, and in the hour when he had shed blood dearer to him than his own, a prayer, the first for years, went up to Heaven from the lips of Reuben Bourne.[79]

The similarities in the methods of Hawthorne and Faulkner have been duly noted; both were literary descendants of Puritan parents. Like Emerson, both took for granted a correlation between the physical and the spiritual. As Richard Fogle says, "Hawthorne habitually saw things allegorically; perception of the equivalence of object and idea was, in harmony with his Puritan

---

[75]Ibid., 287.
[76]Ibid., 282, 283.
[77]Ibid., 281.
[78]Ibid., 287.
[79]Ibid., 270.

heritage, an organic part of his mental makeup. He could not look at a cloud, a fountain, or a cathedral without simultaneously discerning within its shape the emblem of spiritual reality."[80] In spite of Hawthorne's insecurity in setting up allegory, his choice provided him with the same kind of shock value it was to allow O'Connor. In the 1851 preface to *Twice-Told Tales*, Hawthorne describes the effects of using allegory: "Instead of passion, there is sentiment; and even in what purport to be pictures of actual life, we have allegory, not always so warmly dressed in its habiliments of flesh and blood as to be taken into the reader's mind without a shiver."[81] Ursula Brumm, too, notes the efficacy of Hawthorne's method: "In Hawthorne, the reality of thought, idea, and imagination continually interpenetrates physical reality to such an extent that ideas, thought, supersensual things, and even chimeras can exert influence just like real, palpable things."[82] Here Brumm is, of course, making excuses for allegory, stating that in Hawthorne, a system of correspondences and representations has the same force as reality. What she does not acknowledge—which we must note as the foundation for a discussion of Southern literature—is not only the appropriateness of allegory for dealing with issues such as guilt and the conflicts of the heart, but the near inevitability of allegory.

Another critic, John Becker, claims Hawthorne made allegory into a "kind of superior realism."[83] Yet, I would argue, allegory is—in or out of Hawthorne's work—a superior realism; a writer goes to allegory to explore imaginatively the far reaches of the spiritual realm. Becker is correct when he writes that Hawthorne's characters are "not simply abstractions" but are "demonstrations of the fact that distortions of the personality are real, that men can become monodimensional, walking symbols of the diseases that infect human existence."[84] However, as we shall discuss, few modern allegorical characters are monodimensional or flat.

---

[80]Richard Fogle, *Hawthorne's Fiction: The Light and the Dark* (Norman OK: University of Oklahoma Press, 1972) 69.

[81]Quoted by Neal Frank Doubleday, *Hawthorne's Early Tales* (Durham NC: Duke University Press, 1970) 69.

[82]Brumm, *American Thought*, 116.

[83]John E. Becker, *Hawthorne's Historial Allegory: An Examination of the American Conscience* (New York: Kennikat Press, 1971) 176.

[84]Ibid., 176.

Certainly, Hawthorne's use of allegory has its weaknesses. By its very nature, as Bainard Cowain precisely states, "Allegory does not achieve a solution to the crisis that engenders it";[85] it can only point to a higher plane of experience and perception. In his preface to "Rappaccini's Daughter" (1844), Hawthorne himself pointed out another flaw in his "inveterate love of allegory" in that it was "apt . . . to steal away the human warmth out of his conceptions."[86] Allegory often does focus on theme largely to the exclusion of characterization. Its intent is unashamedly, as we shall discover, to relay its message, its moral (although this is not all it accomplishes). Sometimes a moral is achieved at the cost of flesh-and-blood characters and close reader identification. Once again, the purpose of allegory weds itself to the aim of the Puritans as they sought to save human beings from the demons within, and to the convictions of Emerson as he revealed correspondences between natural facts and spiritual concerns.

While Hawthorne chooses biblical imagery and religious terminology to explain the relationship of men and women to their universe, Melville employs allegory to serve a broader purpose. One problem in linking Hawthorne and Melville too closely is revealed in the assessment of Long that the Calvinist imagination they shared "worked against a commitment to realism" and caused them to "regard the physical world as a symbolic chart."[87] Behind such a statement lurk two troublesome assumptions: One is that the Calvinist inheritance of Hawthorne and Melville prevented them from pursuing a "commitment to realism," perhaps to Long a higher cause than the one they accomplished. Second, while both—like Emerson—saw the "physical world as a symbolic chart," they did not share his (or each other's) vision of wholeness in that world. In Emerson's symbolic correspondences one notes a pervasive optimism grounded in the Transcendentalist's conviction of the orderliness and rationality of the cosmos. Often, Hawthorne clung to that vision, for to sin, humankind must sin *against* something, an Order outside of and superior to himself. But for Melville, that Order did not exist, and his allegories were often bitter railings against an absent God.

Even though allegorical devices abound aboard Captain Delano's ship in *Benito Cereno* and Bartleby is the representative victim of an oppressive

---

[85]Bainard Cowain, *Exiled Waters: Moby-Dick and the Crisis of Allegory* (Baton Rouge LA: Louisiana State University Press, 1982) 29.

[86]Quoted by Doubleday, in *Hawthorne's Early Tales*, 62.

[87]Long, *The Great Succession*, 4.

world in "Bartleby the Scrivener," Melville's best allegories are born in *Moby-Dick* and his best short novel, *Billy Budd.* While a thorough examination of *Moby-Dick* as allegory is neither possible here nor necessary, we must look instead at Melville's philosophy of allegory as revealed in these much-discussed works. When Ishmael refers to the white whale as a "hideous and intolerable allegory,"[88] the reader faces neither the development of Ishmael's consciousness nor a furthering of plot. Ishmael is instead a voyager in a foreign world of the spirit, facing for the first time the realization that trusting himself in high Emersonian fashion may lead to courageous self-annihilation. He also survives the thrashings of the Leviathan only to learn that he can interpret his world no more effectively than he can determine the measure of evil and innocence within Moby-Dick. Like the mariner of Samuel Taylor Coleridge's tale, Ahab and Ishmael confront the frailty of human perception. They do not, as Brumm would have us believe, war against the "original evil power to which God allotted a place and function in the world."[89] Could the sailors define their adversary as evil, the quest would be simple. As it is, they war not with principalities but with living things in the murky depths of their own consciousness.

    Moby-Dick may be read as an allegory of the mind, as is *Rime of the Ancient Mariner.* What Ishmael discovers by watching Ahab is that the cosmos preserves no "rightness" of cause-effect. Like the mariner who haphazardly slays an albatross, Ishmael learns that innocence, too, has its own consequences. While the mariner befriends the creatures of the deep and assumes a brotherhood with the "happy living things" of the ocean, Ahab attributes malignant cruelty to the natural actions of Moby-Dick and sets out to avenge himself. The mariner, instead, reveals,

> A spring of love gushed from my heart,
> And I blessed them unaware;
> Sure my kind saint took pity on me,
> And I blessed them unaware.
> The self-same moment I could pray;
> And from my neck so free

---

[88]Quoted by Lawrance Thompson, in *Melville's Quarrel with God* (Princeton NJ: Princeton University Press, 1952) 196.
[89]Brumm, *American Thought,* 179.

The Albatross fell off, and sank
Like lead into the sea.[90]

Whereas the Calvinist world, dark and cruel though it was, promised a God-ordained logic and assured us that good would be rewarded, Melville's world assured us only that no metaphysical system existed and that—as in Coleridge's poem—innocence is as easily punished as deliberate wrongdoing. T. Walter Herbert, Jr., states, "Ishmael joins for a time in Ahab's sharply focused hatred of the divine; his resignation from Ahab's quest is presented as the ultimate skeptical discovery that no coherent Vision of the Truth is possible."[91] Herbert is also correct when he recognizes that Ishmael "passes beyond Ahab's madness" into a "larger sanity."[92] Ishmael discovers that experience corroborates only that there is no structure of the divine in the world. Here, Moby-Dick as symbol conceals as much as it reveals; the signposts of the spiritual that Melville discovered assured him only of the haphazardness of creation.

Yet it was not Melville's saturation with the Bible that determined his manner of relaying truth. Once he moved—like Faulkner, O'Connor, Kafka, and others—into the realm of the spiritual, the whale he conceived became allegory. Queequeg's coffin, the doubloon nailed to the mast, the prophecy of Fedallah, and the wisdom of Starbuck inevitably take on allegorical significance. Melville saves himself from charges of contrivance by the very scope and nature of his literary quest.

Just as the text of *Moby-Dick* confirms Melville's view of an irrational world, *Billy Budd* takes the message one tragic step further. While Ishmael discovers and survives, Budd stands as the ultimate representative of the doomed innocent. Budd, the "stupid natural-Christ," finds himself pitted against Claggart, the "prudently rational Satan," in Kingsley Widmer's analysis of Melville's parable of good versus evil. Yet *good* here has nothing of the wiliness of the serpent advocated even by Christ in the New Testament. Purity of spirit is here ignorance, and it costs Budd both his perception and his life. Budd has often been likened to an innocent Adam or a suffering Christ, but he is—in a peculiar parallel to the strong-witted, tenacious Ahab—trapped in a world he misunderstands and misdefines. Why would Claggart want to hurt

---

[90] *The Norton Anthology*, 2:199.
[91] Herbert, *Moby-Dick and Calvinism*, 92.
[92] Ibid.

him? How could the captain see Claggart's death as anything but an accident? Budd meekly submits himself to the crucifixion scene, a hapless Christ who, though beloved, has had no effect on the system of shipboard justice. Widmer aptly clarifies the remainder of Melville's message when he analyzes Vere's role in the allegory:

> We may thus accept the magisterial and virtuous appearing Vere as the father-God of the allegory, but one in which he functions as an authoritarian whose divinity reveals the larger form of the rationally prudent madness of his plotting servitor, Claggart. [Vere thereby represents] the true father diety as vicious virtue.[93]

If God exists, he is either impotent or willfully detached. Either way, neither Budd nor Melville has any means of appeal.

Southern allegory is linked often and convincingly with the darker vision of Hawthorne and Melville. An explanation of the nature and state of humankind is best accomplished through the symbolic development and representation available in allegory. Humanity's precarious situation in an indecipherable world found sound expression in the parables of Kafka, especially "The Chinese Puzzle." In the parable, a small ball must find its way in a game down "blue labyrinthine paths" to a hole bored in the rich wood. Endowed with a consciousness, the ball expresses its fear that it was not made for the paths: "That was partly true, for indeed the paths could hardly contain it, but it was also untrue, for the fact was that it was very carefully made to fit the width of the paths exactly, but the paths were certainly not meant to be comfortable for it, or else it would not have been a puzzle at all."[94] The beauty of Kafka's parables is that they are not reducible; they are *about* incomprehensibility. To be sure, *Moby-Dick* and *Billy Budd* share the revelation of irrationality with Kafka's parables, as well as the dark vision of the Southern novel.

---

[93]Kingsley Widmer, *The Ways of Nihilism: A Study of Herman Melville's Short Novels* (Los Angeles: California State Colleges, 1970) 29.

[94]*The Complete Stories and Parables* (New York: Book of the Month Club, Inc., 1983) 487.

3. Southern Allegory and the American Myth

Out of the quarrel with others we make rhetoric;
Out of the quarrel with ourselves, poetry.
—W. B. Yeats

In the country districts great numbers of these broken-down Southerners are still to be seen in patched blue-jeans sitting on ancestral fences, shotguns across their laps and hound-dogs at their feet, surveying their unkempt acres while they comment shrewdly on the ways of God.
—John Crowe Ransom
I'll Take My Stand

In the dark mirror there is a dim hollow-eyed Spanish Christ. The pox is spreading on his face. Vacuoles are opening in his chest. It is the new Christ, the sinful Christ. The old Christ died for our sins and it didn't work, we were not reconciled. The new Christ shall reconcile man with his sins. The new Christ lies drunk in a ditch.
—Walker Percy
Love in the Ruins

One cannot deal with Southern novels without a sense of history and an understanding of the Bible, for allusions to both abound. This does not mean, of course, that Southerners write history—any more than Nathaniel Hawthorne did. Neither does it mean that William Faulkner, Flannery O'Connor, or Robert Penn Warren subscribes to the fundamentalist Protestant faith that characterizes the Deep South. What one cannot avoid in Southern literature is the belief that we are fallen people who seek a savior. For Faulkner and Warren, that savior is a political one, one who can point to a new vision and who can redeem history. The savior O'Connor describes must bring grace, forgiveness, and self-awareness to the individual before the culture can be healed.

To understand the Southern writer's message and method, one must turn again to allegory. Richard Fogle, in his book *Hawthorne's Fiction*, writes, "T. S. Eliot has said that good religious poetry teaches us not a doctrine but how it feels to believe it; and so it should be with allegory."[95] Allegory allows us, with O'Connor, to assume the vision of a Roman Catholic who sympathizes and recognizes her link with the wretchedly lost of the earth. When allegory fails, it fails because it requires a reader not only to see "how it feels to believe it," but to believe it. Allegory also suffers when its representations are too blatant and its didacticism too oppressive.

To salvage allegory from the wastebin of second-rate fictional method, one must recognize that allegory can be nothing if not didactic. As we have noted, it excludes what Angus Fletcher calls "action and image" in favor of theme.[96] "Allegory gives point and reference and therefore is in itself a guarantee of purpose,"[97] writes Fogle. Whereas the message of an allegorical novel, such as *The Golden Bowl* (with Henry James' cracked bowl and much-flawed prince), provides a center and helps sustain the action, Fletcher is correct when he asserts that too often "allegory threatens never to end."[98]

An obvious problem for the modernist reader arises when one realizes the truth of another of Fletcher's statements: "Allegory does not possess a Kantian 'disinterest.' "[99] Sallie TeSelle concurs: "An allegory is translucent to its reality—it is a form of direct communication which assumes that the reader or listener already knows about the reality being symbolized."[100] Not only does the reader need to accept (at least temporarily) the theological, historical, or psychological bias or message of an allegorical work, but the reader must immerse himself or herself in an author's preconceptions and sustain a suspension of disbelief. As Fletcher writes,

> Obscurity appears to be a price necessarily paid for the lack of a universal, common doctrinal background. If readers do not share this background with the author, they may still be impressed by the ornaments of the vision, as "mere ornaments," but these will not for such readers have the cosmic reference of true allegorical language.[101]

---

[95]Fogle, *Hawthorne's Fiction*, 7.
[96]Fletcher, *Allegory*, 304.
[97]Fogle, *Hawthorne's Fiction*, 42.
[98]Fletcher, *Allegory*, 367.
[99]Ibid., 322.
[100]TeSelle, *Speaking in Parables*, 77.
[101]Fletcher, *Allegory*, 359.

What is the strength of allegory? An almost magical recreation of a people and a time in an attempt to convince and persuade. "It allows for instruction, for rationalizing, for categorizing and codifying, for casting spells," writes Fletcher. "To conclude, allegories are the natural mirrors of ideology."[102] Allegory is rarely ordered or rational; it sets up, as Fletcher writes, "magical relationships which have only superficially the form of ordered arguments."[103]

In his book *Exiled Waters: Moby-Dick and the Crisis of Allegory*, Bainard Cowain asserts the importance of allegory in a culture clouded in self-doubt:

> Allegory has arisen at moments in history when a people has found itself in a crisis of identity: its members seeing themselves as inheritors of a past tradition of such authority that the tradition is identified with their very name as a people, yet on the other hand finding much of that tradition morally or factually unacceptable.[104]

We have seen the American Puritan look back longingly at his or her biblical heritage; the New Englander moving away from Calvinist ancestors by borrowing their language for the escape; and now we see Southern writers attempting to redefine themselves and their region through biblical imagery and a newly born allegorical world. The culture that resorts to allegory must ally itself with history while defining itself mythically. The Southern myth is not the American myth, for the American Adam—innocent adventurer chosen by God for mighty tasks and great words—steers the national ship. Southern novelists follow in the Puritan tradition, sharing the shadowy world of Hawthorne and Melville, seeking a savior. C. Vann Woodward, in his classic *The Burden of Southern History*, states that the South learned conclusively following the Civil War that it was not the "darling of divine providence."[105] The William Byrd who could rise to prayer, read a passage in Hebrews, and then beat a servant for having locked him out of the house is but one early example of the divided person with whom the Southern writer is obsessed.

---

[102]Ibid., 368.

[103]Ibid., 180.

[104]Cowain, *Exiled Waters*, 11.

[105]C. Vann Woodward, *The Burden of Southern History* (Baton Rouge LA: Louisiana State University Press, 1960) 191.

The South itself is a divided world, for the Southern writer stands in the midst of Atlanta, Birmingham, and Shreveport to plead for an agrarian, conservative, anti-industrial way of life. The Southerner continues, as John Crowe Ransom writes, to identify himself or herself with a "spot of ground."[106] Andrew N. Lytle writes in his essay, *I'll Take My Stand*, the Southerner's agrarian bible, that the Southerner must "close his ears to these heresies that accumulate about his head, for they roll from the tongues of false prophets." "He should know that prophets do not come from cities, promising riches and store clothes. They have always come from the wilderness, stinking of goats and running with lice, and telling of a different sort of treasure, one a corporation head would not understand."[107] The Southerner is encouraged by critics such as Walter Sullivan to cling to a tradition of "good manners . . . and a love of the land and animate sense of mystery."[108] Even W. J. Cash writes in *The Mind of the South*, "Proud, brave, honorable by its lights, courteous, personally generous, loyal, swift to act, often too swift, but signally effective, sometimes terrible, in its action—such was the South at its best. And such at its best it remains today, despite the great falling away in some of its virtues."[109]

The Southern writers in this study continue to uphold and sustain the old values, and it is Cash who best understands that while Southerners are more aware of history—defined as the collective experience of a people—they are also more caught up in a dream of what they hope has been. In his preface, Cash delineates the Old South of the legend:

> It was a sort of stage piece out of the eighteenth century, wherein gesturing gentlemen move soft-spokenly against a background of rose gardens and dueling grounds, through always gallant duels, and lovely ladies, in farthingales, never for a moment lost that exquisite remoteness which has been the dream of all men and the possession of none.[110]

---

[106]John Crowe Ransom, "Reconstructed but Unregenerate," in *I'll Take My Stand: The South and the Agrarian Tradition* (New York: Harper and Brothers, 1930) 19.

[107]Andrew N. Lytle, "The Hind Tit," in ibid., 206.

[108]Walter Sullivan, *Death by Melancholy: Essays on Modern Southern Fiction* (Baton Rouge LA: Louisiana State University Press, 1972) x.

[109]W. J. Cash, *The Mind of the South* (New York: Doubleday, 1954) 425-26.

[110]Ibid., preface.

The New South has not forgotten the dream of community and family, and Cash likens it to a "tree with many age rings, with its limbs and trunk bent and twisted by all the winds of the years, but with its tap root in the Old South."[111] But if suffering produces great literature, then the losses in war and regional identity that the South endured have spawned its literary Renascence. Its losses may help it, as Ransom believes, to prevail. "I believe," he writes, "there is possible no deep sense of beauty, no heroism of conduct, and no sublimity of religion, which is not informed by the humble sense of man's precarious position in the universe."[112]

While the South may be admired for—even emulated in—many of its characteristics, it remains a testimony to our potential for greed, evil, and rationalization. In ten years—from the beginning of 1890 to the close of 1899—1,111 blacks were lynched in the United States. Of the 3,397 lynched from 1882 to 1938, only 366 were murdered outside former Confederate states, and of these 185 were lynched in border states of Maryland, Kentucky, West Virginia, and Missouri—all more than one-half Southern.[113] Mutilation and burning with branding irons were common in slave-holding states. Cash recreates the plantation world of honeysuckle and gracious ladies: "The lash lurked always in the background. Its open crackle could often be heard where field hands were quartered. Into the gentlest houses drifted now and then the sound of dragging chains and shackles, the bay of hounds, the report of pistols on the trail of the runaway."[114] This heart of darkness—what Cash calls "that sadism which lies concealed in the depths of human nature"[115]—ultimately swallowed the whites as well as their slaves. The aristocracy tried to purify slavery by citing biblical excerpts concerning obedience; they tried to describe blacks as children who needed protection.

Most damaging of all was the fact that the South knew of its guilt and had to face its own hypocrisy. Of the 130 abolition societies established before 1827, Cash relates, more than 100 were in the South. The region carried "in its secret heart," he said, "a powerful and uneasy sense of the essential rightness of the nineteenth century's position on slavery."[116] While blacks were

---

[111]Ibid.

[112]Ransom, "Reconstructed but Unregenerate," 10.

[113]Cash, *The Mind of the South*, 301.

[114]Ibid., 94.

[115]Ibid.

[116]Ibid., 73.

composing spirituals and turning to the Christian Messiah, Southern whites were seeking a Deliverer of their own. The Age of Nostalgia and the preservation of romantic fiction began as a way to counter the guilt of slavery and the eventual defeat during the Civil War. The region needed desperately to justify itself to the rest of the world and to itself.

But the woes of the South had only begun. Having lost its farmland to Sherman's March, its few factories and scattered railroads to the Union, and its sons to the superior Northern artillery and arms, the South was to face poverty and backward educational systems in the twentieth century. In 1931, the South produced almost two million bales of cotton, and the foreign crop declined by two million. To the South, the time seemed right for profit. However, a thirteen-million-bale carryover from the previous year brought the world supply to thirty-nine million. The world's annual consumption was only twenty-three million. This "conclusive disaster"[117] leads Cash to say,

> Everybody was either ruined beyond his wildest previous fears or stood in peril of such ruin. . . . Men everywhere walked in a kind of daze. They clustered, at first to assure one another that all would shortly be well; then with the passage of time, to ask questions in the pleading hope of thus being assured; but in the end they fled before the thought in one another's eye.[118]

When the cotton disaster struck, 80 percent of all Southern farms had fewer than 100 acres, so recovery via marketing other produce was impossible. With financial disaster came either resignation or hostility toward the Yankee. Cash writes,

> They had laughed at first, uneasily. But afterward, when they heard from the pulpit that it was a punishment visited upon the people from the hand of God as the penalty of their sins . . . they accepted it in some fashion, and, as always, without demur.[119]

Cash also provides one of the most revealing examples of the Southern religious mind at work. The tale involves a Southern mill worker who, suffering

---

[117]Ibid., 360.
[118]Ibid., 361.
[119]Ibid., 362.

slow loss of hearing and pain in his back from work, also supported a wife, who was spitting blood, and a baby, who had been born mentally ill. How did the man respond to his afflictions? Cash writes, "Quite literally, and in the most unquestioning faith, he thought of them—as his preachers thought of them, and as Southern people at large thought of them—as direct visitations from the hand of God, inexplicable, or explicable only on the hypothesis of sin, and to be borne without complaint."[120]

Walter Sullivan points out that until World War II, the South carried with it both Christianity, which promised deliverance, and slavery, which gnawed at one's conscience. The religious explanation? "We are guilty because everyone has sinned." Now, however, Sullivan reminds us, the "metaphysical framework is gone" and all the terms of the dialectic are changed. "The guilt becomes a secular guilt, with only a secular way to deal with it," he writes, "and the only way a secular society can deal with guilt is to deny the nature of man, to say that man is ultimately perfectible."[121] While Sullivan may be overstating his point—does a person, for example, have to be "perfectible"?—he does come to grips with the inevitability of guilt. However, a shift from a fundamentalist Christian to a humanistic or Transcendentalist view was not to be, and the South became what Lewis Simpson terms the "Republic of the Lost Cause." Unable to do away with guilt, the South began to look for a new kind of savior. It also began to write its own cultural myth, a myth its writers would incorporate into their allegorical portrayals. Simpson writes,

> A society that has failed in war and the shedding of blood to confirm its intellectual interpretation as its own version of the society of history and science seeks its resurrection in a transcendent myth of its existence. A society of mind invents a myth of itself and completes the secularization of the spiritual by spiritualizing itself as a society of myth and tradition.[122]

---

[120]Ibid., 214.

[121]Quoted in *Southern Literary Study: Problems and Possibilities*, eds., Louis D. Rubin, Jr., and C. Hugh Holman (Chapel Hill NC: University of North Carolina Press, 1975) 136.

[122]Lewis Simpson, "The Southern Republic of Letters and *I'll Take My Stand*," in *A Band of Prophets: The Vanderbilt Agrarians after Fifty Years*, eds., William C. Harvard and Walter Sullivan (Baton Rouge LA: Louisiana State University Press, 1982) 81-82.

One of the ways the South had in which to justify itself was its fundamentalist, Protestant faith. Perhaps, the region seemed to believe, we can rewrite our story, emphasize our past strengths, and turn our guilt over to the church. In what Cowain calls a "new sense of allegory,"[123] Southerners began moving away from the "petrified text"[123] of Scripture and embraced the concept of suffering Christ who would lead them to a Final Victory. Tragic heroes of all ages became Christ's brothers—from Billy Budd to Joe Christmas to Kurt Vonnegut's Billy Pilgrim. Ursula Brumm states, "The bitter outbursts of innocent heroes, who often leave an entire world in ruins behind them, would be meaningless if Christ did not lend them the significance of innocence suffering magnificently."[124] Rejecting the Puritan Old Testament emphasis, Southern Protestants began to concentrate on the gentle, merciful Christ who helps the oppressed. The new portrait of God as represented in Christ, of course, made its way into Southern allegorical novels, including *Love in the Ruins* and *Second Coming* by Walker Percy.

In Percy's portrayals of the "Christ-forgetting Christ-haunted death-dealing Western world,"[125] characters watch and wait for signs of apocalypse, the return of Christ, and the advent of eternity. Here lies deliverance from human frailty, from guilt, from poverty. *Second Coming* traces the search of Will Barrett of Linwood, North Carolina, who seeks desperately for sign of the divine. Leaving home to look for God and a prophecy of apocalypse, Will meets Allie, recently released from a mental institution. The sign he awaits is death; what he discovers is that he longs for life and community. At one point in the narrative, Will cries,

> Speak, God, or be silent. And if you're silent, I'll understand that.
> O ye mystics who go out in the desert and see visions, o ye old men who dream dreams, who believes you?
> O ye suicides who go not so gently into that good nothing, you can't tell me either. But I've beat you both. In either case I'll know.

---

[123]Cowain, *Exiled Waters*, 20.
[124]Brumm, *American Thought*, 219.
[125]Walker Percy, *Love in the Ruins: The Adventures of a Bad Catholic at a Time Near the End of the World* (New York: Farrar, Straus, & Giroux, 1971) 3.

> Speak, God, and let me know if the Jews are a sign and
> the Last Days are at hand. . . .
>   If you do not speak and the Jews are not a sign, then that
> too is an answer of sorts. It means that what is at hand are not the
> Last Days but only the last days, my last days, a minor event, to be
> sure, but an event of importance to me.[126]

Having asked a priest about Christ's return, Will brings about his own moment of epiphany: "What is it I want from her and him [Allie and the priest], he wondered, not only want but must have? Is she a gift and therefore a sign of a giver? Could it be that the Lord is here, masquerading behind this simple silly holy face? Am I crazy to want both, her and Him? No, not want, must have. And will have."[127] Allie takes on a Messianic role in Will's mind, and Christ thereby fully takes on human form.

However, Percy describes Will not as a Southerner but as an isolated American who has won financial security at the expense of soul. "Death in this century is not the death people die but the death people live,"[128] Percy writes. Shot at by a poacher, Will lies unharmed in the woods, "speculating on the odd upside-downness of the times, that on a beautiful Sunday in Old Carolina, it takes a gunshot to restore a man to himself."[129] Percy describes Will as he later considers suicide in a pessimistic survey of his past: "There he sat in the same Mercedes, a 450 SEL 6.9-liter sedan, a badly flawed frazzled shakey American, as hollow-eyed as a Dachau survivor, still smelling of cave crud, in a perfect German machine redolent of leather, polished wood, and fine oil on steel."[130] Through Will, one sees both the displaced man and the culture riddled with and incapacitated by self-doubt.

If one considers the myth of innocence and opulence Americans hide behind, it quickly becomes obvious that the fictional world of *Love in the Ruins* and *Second Coming* is the world of the South—the world Americans seek to ignore. Woodward sets up the contrast between America and the South in three major areas: (1) the economic abundance of America versus Southern

---

[126]Walker Percy, *The Second Coming* (New York: Farrar, Straus, & Giroux, 1980) 212-13.

[127]Ibid., 360.

[128]Ibid., 271.

[129]Ibid., 18.

[130]Ibid., 268-69.

poverty (In 1880 the per capita wealth of the South—based on estimated true valuation of property—was $376, as opposed to $1,186 in all other states.); (2) the American myth of success and invincibility versus the Southern losses in economic, social, and political arenas; (3) the myth of American innocence versus the "tortured conscience of the South."[131] America stands unique among nations as one country that overcomes all obstacles by "luck, by abundant resources, by ingenuity, by technology, by organizing cleverness, or by sheer force of arms."[132] History cannot hurt us. As God's chosen people (Thomas Jefferson proposed a picture of the children being led out of Israel as a national seal), we are set apart from the suffering of the rest of the world. During the Vietnam War, the world began to suspect a "deeper commitment to American pride than to Vietnamese freedom." Like the South, Woodward adds, we have chosen in the face of criticism of our economic system to defend capitalism "to the point of attack."[133]

Theologian Reinhold Niebuhr notes the link between the Calvinists, Jeffersonians, and modern-day Americans who see "complete compatibility between virtue and prosperity," and he expresses the unspoken sentiment of presidents during annual Thanksgiving proclamations: "They have congratulated God on the virtues and ideals of the American people, which have so well merited the blessings of prosperity we enjoy."[134] John Crowe Ransom reinforces the ideas of Percy, Woodward, and Niebuhr when he writes that "Americans are still dreaming the materialistic dreams of their youth": "The stuff these dreams were made on was the illusion of preeminent personal success over a material opposition. Their tone was belligerance and the euphemism under which it masqueraded was ambition. But men are not lovely, and men are not happy, for being too ambitious."[135] Only in America, writes Sacvan Bercovitch, has free enterprise been given the "halo of grace."[136]

If the South shrouds itself in the graveclothes of guilt and watches its past over its shoulder, where does the rest of America stand? R. W. B. Lewis's

---

[131]Woodward, *The Burden of Southern History*, 16-20.

[132]Ibid., 188.

[133]Ibid., 219, 203-204.

[134]Reinhold Niebuhr, *The Irony of American History* (New York: Charles Scribner's Sons, 1952) 51-53.

[135]Ransom, "Reconstructed but Unregenerate," 8-9.

[136]Sacvan Bercovitch, *The American Jeremiad* (Madison WI: University of Wisconsin Press, 1978) 141.

American Adam is but one answer, as the young American nation chooses Adam, the innocent, as a symbol. The United States as a whole, what Percy terms the "apple of God's eye,"[137] becomes moral arbiter of the world in spite of its capitalism and closet imperialism. Percy writes in *Love in the Ruins*, "The U. S. A. didn't work! Is it even possible that from the beginning it never did work? That the thing always had a flaw in it, a place where it would shear, and that all this time we were not really different from Ecuador and Bosnia-Herzegovina, just richer."[138] Instead of seeking a Messiah, America decided to establish itself as the savior of the world. Our messianic dream, Niebuhr states, lies in that we consider ourselves not as "potential masters" but as "tutors of mankind in its pilgrimage to perfection."[139] This superiority is possible only for a nation that stands undefeated in war and that boasts of its churches by sending its missionaries to the far corners of the earth to spread its own particular gospel. As the bastion of morality, we may see ourselves as Woodward reveals, as "morally obliged to liberate the enslaved peoples of the earth, punish the wicked oppressor, and convert the liberated peoples to our way of thought."[140] A fictional perspective is provided by Melville in *White-Jacket*:

> And we Americans are the peculiar chosen people—the Israel of our time; we bear the ark of the liberties of the world. God has predestined, mankind expects, great things from our race; and great things we feel in our souls. The rest of the nations must soon be in our rear. We are the pioneers of the world; the advance-guard, sent on through the wilderness of untried things, to break a new path in the New World that is ours. . . . Long enough have we been skeptics with regard to ourselves, and doubted whether, indeed, the political Messiah had come. But he has come in *us*, if we would but give utterance to his promptings.[141]

---

[137]Percy, *Love in the Ruins*, 57.

[138]Ibid., 56.

[139]Niebuhr, *The Irony of American History*, 71.

[140]Woodward, *The Burden of Southern History*, 206.

[141]Herman Melville, *Romances of Herman Melville* (New York: Tudor Publishing, 1931) 1199.

One of the most provocative books dealing with the American sense of destiny is Bercovitch's *The American Jeremiad.* Bercovitch, a Canadian immigrant, finds himself astonished by a "population that, despite its bewildering mixture of race and creed, could believe in something called an American mission, and could invest that patent fiction with all the emotional, spiritual, and intellectual appeal of a religious quest."[142] Nationalism and religion become one, as America sees itself as the "new chosen people, city on a hill, promised land, destined progress, New Eden, American Jerusalem."[143] The American Revolution was a kind of escape from Egypt; imperialism, a holy war. Bercovitch writes,

> It would be another generation or so before this typology of mission could be fully rendered—before Washington could be enshrined as Savior . . . the Declaration of Independence adequately compared to the Sermon on the Mount . . . the Constitution duly ordained (in Emerson's words) as "the best book in the world" next to the New Testament.[144]

American national destiny, Niebuhr writes, became "God's effort to make a new beginning in the history of mankind."[145] How could the new Eden come to a bad end? How could its exploits be anything but sanctioned by God? And what would be the effects of such a view on national literature? In her book, *American Thought and Religious Typology,* Brumm says,

> Actually it seems to be a paradox to speak of a "tragic American hero." Can there be such a thing as an openly confessed tragic world view in American literature? . . . A literature that is acknowledged to be democratic, of a nation with an optimistic belief in life, cannot openly affirm the tragic experience of life. If tragic problems are encountered nonetheless, a situation arises where a redeemer is needed and Christ is summoned in to aid.[146]

---

[142]Bercovitch, *The American Jeremiad,* 11.
[143]Ibid., 92.
[144]Ibid., 129.
[145]Niebuhr, *The Irony of American History,* 4.
[146]Brumm, *American Thought,* 217.

But how often is Christ summoned as the American moves West? As the American Adam stakes his claim and asserts his values as Truth? As—even in *Winesburg, Ohio* and other novels of the American way—a young innocent prevails?

Perhaps herein lies the reason Southern short stories and novels are often taught in a course on American literature but are not integrated into it. How does one mesh the two visions? The gap between Ralph Waldo Emerson and Walt Whitman and William Faulkner and Flannery O'Connor is astonishingly wide, for the South cannot affirm a way of life it has lost. Its history is one of European aristocratic hope exploded in sin. Percy writes in *Love in the Ruins*, "One little test: here's a helpless man in Africa, all you have to do is not violate him. That's all."[147] Failing in this and other trials, the South blusters in the dark, and its writers move back into the biblical Eden—the first Garden—and relive their culture's fall from grace time and time again. Attempts to rewrite the past look strangely the same, as over and over a failed messiah dies his troubled death. Certain of the flaw within us, certain of the evil that we cannot obliterate around us, the Southern writer unravels a new myth. No one goes West. Wins battles. Becomes wealthy (even before disaster strikes, as in *The Great Gatsby*). The Southern novel—when it is taught in an American literature course—is an anachronistic piece, an oddity that remains a testimony to a peculiar collective mind.

Niebuhr suggests the following:

> The ironic elements in American history can be overcome, in short, only if American idealism comes to terms with the limits of all human striving, the fragmentariness of all human wisdom, the precariousness of all historic configurations of power, and the mixture of good and evil in all human virtue.[148]

The Southern writer knows this lesson and seeks to endure and prevail in its shadow. Having looked into the abyss of their own natures, Southern novelists seek a savior; for the Southern writer, self-reliance remains but a fantasy, a Camelot that melts in the rain. Humankind cannot understand, much less rescue, itself. Ransom is correct when he writes,

---

[147]Percy, *Love in the Ruins*, 57.
[148]Niebuhr, *The Irony of American History*, 133.

It is out of fashion in these days to look backward rather than forward. About the only American given to it is some unreconstructed Southerner, who persists in his regard for a certain terrain, a certain history, and a certain inherited way of living. He is punished as his crime deserves. He feels himself in the American scene as an anachronism, and knows he is felt by his neighbors as a reproach.[149]

The Southern novelist has written a new myth of the human condition. Defeat, a sense of sin, a longing for redemption, and a desire for healing set the Southern novel apart, as allegory becomes the most effective method to relay a people's fall from grace. But perhaps its picture of the universe is closer to the Puritan message concerning humanity than we want to admit. Woodward writes,

After Faulkner, Wolfe, Warren, and Welty, no literate Southerner could remain unaware of his heritage or doubt its enduring value. After this outpouring it would seem more difficult than ever to deny a Southern identity, to be "merely American." To deny it would be to deny American participation in a heritage and a dimension of historical experience that America very much needs, a heritage that is far more closely in line with the common lot of mankind than the national legends of opulence and success and innocence.[150]

All four novels we shall explore portray the individual as fallen, having turned his or her back on the divine potential for nobility and compassion. Ike McCaslin of *Go Down, Moses* fails the central moral test in "Delta Autumn," and in the final chapter of the same novel, Gavin Stevens, golden hope of the New South, demonstrates that he, too, has missed the lessons of history. *Light in August* balances the despair and death of Joe Christmas with the emerging self-awareness of Gail Hightower, who suffers his way into a personal Promised Land. *Wise Blood* is an allegory of blindness and of the confrontation between Haze Motes and Jesus, the "ragged figure who moves from tree to tree in the

---

[149]Ransom, "Reconstructed but Unregenerate," 1.
[150]Woodward, *The Burden of Southern History*, 25.

back of his mind."[151] John Singer of *The Heart Is a Lonely Hunter* finds himself the appointed leader of a self-appointed band of disciples and flees his impossible role through isolation and eventual suicide. In the Southern novel, suffering becomes the lot of the individual; the fleeting glimpse of one's face in a mirror, one's only reward.

---

[151]Flannery O'Connor, *Wise Blood* (New York: New American Library, 1962) 2.

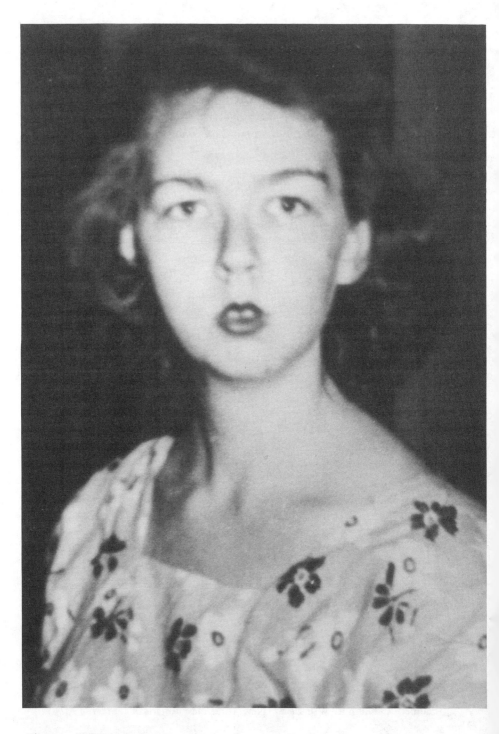

Flannery O'Connor

Photo courtesy Flannery O'Connor Collections, Ina Dillard Russell Library, Milledgeville, Georgi

Chapter 2

Allegory and Christianity
in the Modern South

1. The Problem of Allegory

Unlike other writers the allegorist has elected a literary form that does not readily carry conviction except for those readers who live in a particular era and have at least an inner awareness of those problems with which the allegorist is dealing. It is no accident that the best allegorists have written in ages of comprehensive spiritual speculation, or when such introspection seemed exigent: Dante in the Middle Ages, Bunyan in the Puritan period, Hawthorne and Melville during nineteenth-century American Transcendentalism, and Kafka in the twentieth-century Europe.[1]

> —Edward A. Bloom
> "The Allegorical Principle"

Allegory has not completely lived down the reputation it achieved in the nineteenth century. From being a dominant literary form in the Renaissance, allegory fell into critical disrepute. Critics such as Edwin Honig have gone a long way in defending it, but there is little doubt that since the Romantics, some have viewed allegory as a lesser form of literature. The primary reason, as mentioned earlier, is its didactic intent. Also noted earlier is the tendency of poorly written allegory to focus on simplistic personification and allusion or

---

[1]Edward A. Bloom "The Allegorical Principle," *Journal of English Literary History* 18 (September 1951): 189-90.

to set up a limp hero and chart that hero through a maze of even more limp tests of courage. When *The Faerie Queen* and *Pilgrim's Progress* are lauded as art, they often are treated as superb allegorical accidents or explained away as products of a mind that could not fail no matter what its chosen genre or technique. This chapter, therefore, has three intents: (1) to single out allegory as a form obsessed with metaphysical issues; (2) to defend it as containing the symbols some critics have determined to be its antithesis; and (3) to show why the Southern writer might choose to employ it.

Certainly, not all critics demean allegory. C. S. Lewis, for example, while largely upholding the verdict of Samuel Taylor Coleridge concerning the distinctions between symbol and allegory, writes: "Allegory in some sense, belongs not to medieval man but to man, or even to mind, in general. It is of the very nature of thought and language to represent what is immaterial in picturable terms."[2] Some critics see allegory as deriving from myth and ritual.[3] However, one's success in reading allegory often stems from a recognition of our need to make abstractions concrete and a cultivated ability to suspend one's own political or religious views when reading a work that proposes a specific perspective. Certainly, one cannot ignore the allegorist's commitment to a moral or message. Maureen Quilligan describes the difference between fiction and allegory by saying, "Fiction may only entertain. But all allegorists . . . aim at redemption."[4] She contends, also, that most allegorists incorporate the Bible into their work;[5] while this may be a generalization, it is often true in Southern fiction and reinforces the final goal of allegory: teaching.

---

[2]C. S. Lewis, *Allegory of Love: A Study in Medieval Tradition* (London: Oxford University Press, 1938) 44.

[3]Edwin Honig is one of the critics who provides allegory with a laudable parentage. In *Dark Conceit: The Making of Allegory* (Evanston IL: Northwestern University Press, 1959), he writes, "The literary form called allegory follows through the ages the imperatives of conflicting ideals rooted in the nature of thought and belief. . . . Myth and philosophy give allegory its themes and method; epic and drama prefigure its form; a traditional poetics defines its purpose; and religious doctrines ritualize it in heuristic formulas" (30). Gay Clifford couples myth and allegory as vehicles for what she calls an "inherited belief about the historical past and the structure of the cosmos," in *The Transformations of Allegory* (Boston: Routledge and Kegan Paul, 1974) 66.

[4]Maureen Quilligan, *The Language of Allegory* (Ithaca NY: Cornell University Press, 1979) 64.

[5]Ibid., 96.

For some critics, allegory is thinly disguised dogma that the modern reader has intellectually outrun. For some, it involves not a willing suspension of disbelief, but a willing suspension of all mental effort. Second, critics who follow in the nineteenth-century tradition regarding allegory may assume that a respect for allegory must be based on being oblivious to the modern conclusions concerning language. For allegory to be taken seriously, language must be stable. X must equal X, they propose; the word must mean what it says, since allegory is thought to be a one-to-one correspondence in which the Word is revered. Such critics allow no room for the realization that the reverberations of language are possible in allegory just as in other genres, as we shall see through study of symbol and metaphor. Problems with allegory, claims Gay Clifford, move beyond the moralism of the genre to the fact that allegory is "abstract, speculative, and discursive."[6] Louis MacNeice titles a book *Varieties of Parable* because *allegory* is a word "to which many people today are allergic."[7] Edwin Honig notes the "pervasive feeling against allegory" and says that critics "scorn" it as a "pedestrian notion somehow attached to a few masterworks by which it got in through the back door of literature."[8] Why did the general sentiment against allegory in the nineteenth century develop? Which charges are valid and which exaggerated? Why is the Southerner constructing allegories when only a few other writers—such as Henry James, D. H. Lawrence, Franz Kafka, George Orwell—seem interested in a similar task?

The answer lies on the other side of a war of semantics, for to understand allegory, one must be able to distinguish it from terms often linked or confused with it: symbol, symbolism, metaphor, typology, and parable. Confusion concerning allegory and parable may be bypassed quickly in spite of the critical quicksand, for allegory is often ethereal, rarified, and surreal (as in *Billy Budd, House of the Seven Gables,* and *The Scarlet Letter*), while parable deals with the commonplace (as in the illustrations Jesus used, such as "The Prodigal Son" and "The Lost Sheep," or Kafka's "An Imperial Message"). Kafka's parables are not reducible, for they are about incomprehensibility. In allegory, the abstract idea is dominant in the image—as with "Lady Truth" who redeems the countryside—while in parable, the idea is subordinate. In

---

[6]Clifford, *The Transformations of Allegory,* 7.

[7]Louis MacNeice, *Varieties of Parable* (Cambridge: Cambridge University Press, 1965) i.

[8]Honig, *Dark Conceit,* 3.

"The Prodigal Son," for example, prodigality is predicated on the rebel son's humanity, becoming unessential to the tale. The human (though not always realistic) element becomes the focus, and the parable also does not require association to deduce meaning: it is itself what it is talking about. Both forms, of course, reach toward an ethical lesson as readers are, as Sallie TeSelle writes, "shocked into a new awareness,"[9] another form of violence. Allegory also is defined by many as extended parable; what cannot be praised is the contention of many that allegory is extended metaphor.

Lurking within the literary disputes of the nineteenth century lies the seed of the controversy, for it is with Coleridge that allegory is dismissed as symbolism takes the throne. While the reaction of the Romantics against didacticism and mechanical verse must be recorded and acknowledged as long overdue, their lines between symbol and allegory were made too swiftly and too neatly. Basically, Coleridge and others believed that symbol was rich and unified and an almost magical creation of the Imagination, while allegory was the pedantic child of fancy. His reverence for symbol was born in his study of Scripture, as he found Christ, the cross, and other signposts of the Church complex and explosive in connotation. Second, he viewed allegory as a too-stable system of correspondences used to a didactic and often unjustified end. Coleridge would not have quibbled with C. S. Lewis, for example, who describes some allegory as "stereotyped monotony."[10] Even critics sympathetic to writers of allegory have berated it for simplistic correspondences.[11]

---

[9]Sallie TeSelle, *Speaking in Parables: A Study in Metaphor and Theology* (Philadelphia: Fortress Press, 1975) 13.

[10]Lewis, *The Allegory of Love*, 232.

[11]Miles Orvell, for example, while speaking favorably of *Wise Blood*, casts remaining allegories into a negative light. In *Invisible Parade* (Philadelphia: Temple University Press, 1972), he writes, "But neither is *[Wise Blood]* an allegory in the traditional sense, for it attempts to render an image of experience that is more complex than that of the traditional allegory and that cannot be so easily translated, at every point, into its theological or dogmatic equivalent" (92). Critics such as Richard Fogle and Gay Clifford, who explain why allegory has been consistently underestimated, support the genre. In *Hawthorne's Fiction: The Light and the Dark* (Norman OK: University of Oklahoma Press, 1952), Fogle writes, "We assume that allegory subordinates everything to a pre-determined conclusion: that allegory, in short, is a dishonest counterfeit of literary value" (7). Speaking primarily of critics and writers of the nineteenth century, Clifford describes allegory in *The Transformations of Allegory* as a

It is in *The Statesman's Manual* and in *Miscellaneous Criticism* that we find direct references to Coleridge's view of symbolism and allegory (metaphor). Coleridge writes, "Now an Allegory is but a translation of abstract notions into a picture-language which is itself nothing but an abstraction from objects of the senses; the principal being more worthless even than its phantom proxy, both alike unsubstantial, and the former shapeless to boot."[12] Here Coleridge gives birth to the notion that has become a part of the modern sensibility; allegory is not readable, for it equates a nebulous idea with a nebulous image. Allegory, simply, is flailed for being too concrete—to the point of dulling the mind with simplistic parallels—and for not being concrete enough. The remainder of Coleridge's explanation raises as many questions as it answers, but it leaves no doubt concerning the supremacy of the symbol. Coleridge writes, "On the other hand a Symbol is characterized by a translucence of the Special in the Individual or of the General in the Especial or of the Universal in the General. Above all by the translucence of the Eternal through and in the Temporal."[13] Twice in *The Statesman's Manual* Coleridge explains symbol as being part of the Universal, as integral as a blade of grass to Nature. Symbol, he writes, "always partakes of the Reality which it renders intelligible; and while it enunciates the whole, abides itself as a living part in that Unity, of which it is the representative."[14] In Appendix C, Coleridge adds, "By a symbol I mean, not a metaphor or allegory or any other figure of speech or form of fancy, but an actual and essential part of that, the whole of which it represents."[15]

What emerges from the reactions of the critics such as Coleridge and Edgar Allan Poe, however, is that their personal literary crusade against didacticism found a silent victim in allegory and that they never acknowledged the role symbols may themselves play in allegory. Many modern critics and writers, with the almost universal exception of Southern writers, have separated

---

"matter of imposition: it curbs the freedom of the writer and imposes on the reader to the point of bullying or boredom" (117).

[12] *The Statesman's Manual* in *Lay Sermons*, ed. R. J. White, vol. 6 of *The Collected Works of Samuel Taylor Coleridge*, ed. Kathleen Coburn, Bollingen Series, 75 (Princeton NJ: Princeton University Press, 1972) 30.

[13] *The Statesman's Manual*, in *Lay Sermons*, in *The Collected Works of Samuel Taylor Coleridge*, 30.

[14] Ibid., 30.

[15] Ibid., 79.

allegory and symbolism, without recognizing the productive relationship possible between them.[16] Nonetheless, the critical weight certainly is on Coleridge's side; solitary is the critic who made no distinction between allegory and symbol. Yet when one deals with allegory as, yes, a preconceived system with, yes, a given resolution (often a moral, philosophical, or religious truth), it is not necessary to assume a linear development or a restrictive method. Allegory, we shall see, makes use of the symbols, motifs, and imagery that are part of symbolic structures as well. The division between symbol and allegory is not as simple as Poe would have us believe. In a review of Nathaniel Hawthorne's *Twice-Told Tales* (1847), Poe writes that Hawthorne is "peculiar and not original. . . . He is infinitely too fond of allegory, and can never hope for popularity so long as he persists in it."[17] He says in sum, "In defense of allegory . . . there is scarcely one respectable word to be said."[18] Allegory, as one might expect from Poe, was charged with two unpardonables: the contrivances of didacticism and the "sin of extreme length."[19] One may react to Poe's charges and his comments that *Pilgrim's Progress* is "ludicrously overrated"[20] with a chuckle, but one must, at the same time, acknowledge him as but one in a literary majority.

Dominant critics such as Richard Chase and Charles Feidelson, Jr., defend themselves more specifically and convincingly than Poe, yet they decry allegory for its oversimplification while oversimplifying their own definitions and distinctions concerning the novel. In *The American Novel and Its Tradition*, Chase calls the *A* in *The Scarlet Letter* a "relatively simple sign," a

---

[16]Charles Feidelson, Jr., whose views are discussed in depth in this section, notes that "Like Emerson, Melville used [the words *allegory* and *symbol*] interchangeably, and they meant for him what we ordinarily mean by the latter, in *Symbolism and American Literature* (Chicago: University of Chicago Press, 1953) 326. In an article entitled "Christ and the Christ Figure in American Fiction," *The Christian Scholar* 47 (1964) 118, Robert Detweiler says allegory damaged its credibility as a purveyor of symbols because it was used for too long to relay "religious or political propaganda." Allegory generally is considered a debased symbolism, which uses narrative only to impose a moral lesson.

[17]"Hawthorne's Tales," in *The Shock of Recognition*, ed. Edmund Wilson (New York: Farrar, Straus, and Cudahy, 1943) 168-69.

[18]Ibid., 159.

[19]Ibid., 163.

[20]Ibid., 159.

dangerous claim to make of any image, metonymical or metaphorical. The *A*, he explains, does not succeed, for it stands like an equation for adultery or the "inevitable taint on all human life."[21] Even here, however, Chase has delineated two meanings, one literal and one representative. He has also omitted the perceptions of (1) Pearl, for whom the letter may as easily represent security as guilt; (2) Dimmesdale, for whom the letter may represent cowardice, betrayal, adultery, or shame (or all four); (3) Hester herself, for whom the letter shifts in meaning as she is alternately horrified by and reconciled to it; and (4) the townspeople, for whom the letter may stand for "adultery" or "angel." "Being an ordinary symbol," writes Chase, "the scarlet A is thus suitable to its allegorical context."[22] Melville's whale, he asserts, is "much more complex" and therefore successful.[23]

Chase has missed the point. Justifying an image on the basis of the number of meanings is ignoring the central issue: without intending it, Chase has asserted the role the letter *A* and the whale play as symbols in the works. Allegory, then, may be more compelling and more challenging in one work than in another, but it employs and develops symbols no matter how rich in implication. Again, the spokesman for the majority, Chase states, "In allegory the signs or symbols have little or no existence apart from their paraphrasable meaning. Allegory flourishes best, of course, when everyone agrees on what truth is, when literature is regarded as exposition, not as discovery."[24] But one easily can dispute Chase's contention that allegory is a "language of static signs"[25] that rule out discovery. One system may involve more signifiers (symbols), but all good allegory involves some.

Feidelson, too, bases much of his definition and condemnation of allegory on Hawthorne, whom he does acknowledge as an occasional symbolist "in spite of himself."[26] He, like Chase, distinguishes Hawthorne's work from *Moby-Dick*; in the latter, Feidelson claims, Melville avoids allegory by locating his symbols in a "unitary act of perception."[27] Hawthorne, however, balked at

---

[21]Richard Chase, *The American Novel and Its Tradition* (Baltimore: Johns Hopkins University Press, 1957) 80.

[22]Ibid.

[23]Ibid.

[24]Ibid., 81-82.

[25]Ibid., 81.

[26]Feidelson, *Symbolism and American Literature*, 9.

[27]Ibid., 32.

using symbol, Feidelson contends: "On the one hand, the symbol was valuable precisely because it transcended analytic thought; on the other hand, that very transcendence, with its suggestion of the unconventional, the novel, the disorderly, was potentially dangerous."[28] Feidelson then defines allegory as the "brake that Hawthorne applied to sensibility": "For allegory *was* analytic: allegory was safe because it preserved the conventional distinction between thought and things."[29] Allegory, he concludes, "imposes the pat moral and the simplified character."[30]

Certainly, the problems with allegory have developed, for the form once functioned properly on multiple levels: fictional (entertainment), religious, political, philosophical. But since the eighteenth century, as Edward Bloom points out, allegory has been "decried . . . for tediousness, lack of interest and vagueness."[31] Of the nineteenth century, Bloom summarizes,

> Allegory for Wordsworth . . . is a tastelessly uninspired mode of communication derived from experience and the rational understanding rather than from the lofty vision and imagination to which both Blake and Coleridge aspired . . . [E]sthetic judgment is beginning seriously to supplant the didactic, and such a patently didactic form as allegory is inevitably doomed to condemnation.[32]

One may easily counter that most literature is didactic, if not in intent, perhaps in reception. Even a short story such as "The Cask of Amontillado" by the anti-didactic Poe—written, if he remained true to his high purpose, to provide pleasure alone—may be interpreted as a tale of the pitfalls of hatred and revenge. Nonetheless, the trouble with allegory does not stop even here, for a few overzealous critics such as Clifford compensate too heartily for allegory. Emphasizing that allegory is narrative and that it is one of the more structured modes of writing (since it works toward a conclusion), Clifford writes, "It is this process which symbols on their own cannot express, for symbols are primarily static and allegory is kinetic."[33]

---

[28]Ibid., 14.
[29]Ibid., 14-15.
[30]Ibid., 15.
[31]Bloom, "The Allegorical Principle," 163.
[32]Ibid., 186.
[33]Clifford, *The Transformations of Allegory*, 12.

Symbols, of course, are in no way static, and what Coleridge and others have convincingly asserted is how valuable symbols are to any literary process. This study argues, in fact, not that symbols are lesser than metaphor or allegory, but that they contribute immeasurably to the latter, simply because they *are* kinetic. J. Robert Barth describes Dante as a poet not of allegory but of symbol, "trafficking not with fixities and definites but with mystery."[34] Yet Southern allegorists have promoted nothing if not mystery (a collection of Flannery O'Connor's essays is, in fact, entitled *Mystery and Manners*). Carson McCullers, O'Connor, and William Faulkner ask no questions if not metaphysical ones. Their continual, almost predictable, return to Scripture testifies to a longing to know the mysteries of creation and the nature of humanity. Surely *Pilgrim's Progress* and *The Faerie Queen*, too, rise above fixities and definites; they are far from dogmatic tracts advocating a set and sterile behavior, religious or political.

There are differences between symbol and allegory, but few have delved deeply enough in the semantic jungle to discover them. Interestingly enough, it is Barth who most clearly defines metaphor and symbol:

> In a metaphor we are aware first of the differences between the referents ("My Luve," the "red, red rose"), and come to see some quality or qualities common to them. In symbol we are aware first of the unity (Eliot's rose, Yeats's tree or tower), and only gradually become aware of its complexity.[35]

Allegory may employ both metaphor and symbol. For example, Joanna Burden—as indicated by her name—carries a weight. It is not labelled "Sin," for a modern reader is not likely to tolerate John Bunyan in the pages of a Faulkner novel, but it is a burden. On a figurative level, the burden may be a psychological pregnancy—the guilt born of years of slaveholding, the spinsterhood Faulkner seems to find so appalling, or a sense of personal failure. The same applies to *The Heart Is a Lonely Hunter* and *Wise Blood*, in which Singer is a deaf mute and Haze Motes is blind. The metaphorical correlation becomes immediately clear, yet it is the irony implicit in Singer's deafness and inability to speak that captivates the reader, and it is Haze's ability to see his

---

[34]J. Robert Barth, *The Symbolic Imagination: Coleridge and the Romantic Tradition* (Princeton NJ: Princeton University Press, 1977) 109.

[35]Ibid., 29.

own spiritual blindness that holds our attention. Singer is not deaf, for he is the only one who listens, and he is not unable to speak, for he exudes love and affirmation to those he meets. Haze, the creation of the Catholic mind, believes he must be physically blind in order to heal his spiritual sightlessness. The biblical implications are obvious.

Coleridge is, undoubtedly, correct in setting up a distinction between allegory and symbol. As Honig explains that distinction, allegory is set up consciously, while with symbol, the truth may be unconsciously in the writer's mind.[36] Yet this is always true of symbol, and allegory provides merely a linear structure for the multiple possibilities of symbol. One function is mechanical, and one is organic. Allegory is by nature didactic, yet symbol frees it to meet other criteria as well. Because of symbol, allegory then provides the reader with pleasure and the opportunity to decipher its multiple "truths"—some intended, some not. To retaliate against the message of allegory and miss the symbolic qualities is to sell the genre short. When the two have been divorced, then Sacvan Bercovitch is correct: "Allegory originates, as a rule, in an orthodox, absolute design, and proceeds from the abstract to the particular. Symbolism starts in subjective interpretation, and leads from the discrete to the universal."[37] Symbol, Ursula Brumm explains, begins in reality (Coleridge's unity of image), while allegory is already abstracted from the world.[38] It is, simply, the product of a moral or ethical mind, a perspective, imposed on the work from outside nature or the natural symbolic development of a text. As Clifford writes, "It would be ridiculous to say that symbolism is impossible without narrative: of allegory it would be true."[39]

Not all critics, certainly, have tarred and feathered allegory, as we have seen. Northrop Frye, while acknowledging that the explicit statement of allegory frustrates a modern reader used to irony and paradox, separates naive allegory (used for educational and political purposes) from other forms. He adds, "But even continuous allegory is still a structure of images [symbols], not of disguised ideas, and commentary has to proceed with it exactly as it does with all other literature, trying to see what precepts and examples are suggested

---

[36]Honig, *Dark Conceit*, 46.

[37]*The American Puritan Imagination*, ed. Sacvan Bercovitch (New York: Cambridge University Press, 1974) 10.

[38]Ursula Brumm, *American Thought and Religious Typology* (New Brunswick NJ: Rutgers University Press, 1970) 8.

[39]Clifford, *The Transformations of Allegory*, 14.

by the imagery as a whole."[40] Frye then asserts all commentary as "allegorical interpretation" and defines all literature as "potential allegory of events and ideas."[41] Allegory is an unrealistically comforting form for many. Clifford writes that the effect of symbolism may be fragmentation, while this is not the case with allegory.[42] Clifford clearly has overlooked Franz Kafka, with his riveting allegories of incomprehensibility. Allegory is not the easy way out; the soul-wrenching of other literary forms is present here, too, and a moral ending is not synonymous with a conclusion or resolution.

But what of the twentieth century? Why should critics champion a cause that has encountered so much opposition? The answer remains partially that there is room for allegory, yet it must change as all other forms have done. No Southerner is rewriting *Pilgrim's Progress* as Pierre Menard rewrote *Don Quixote*. Modern allegory has lost its hero, retained the importance of character within plot, resisted the urge to recreate (though it continues to allude to) mythical or biblical characters (even Christ), and no longer necessarily supports the religious or political structure of the day.[43]

Perhaps modern literature has reentered an allegorical age; a defensible argument may be set forth that the South never left it. Bloom is one of the few critics who have linked the failure of allegory with cultural literary preferences. By doing so, he clearly sets up a reason for allegory to have thrived in the South, although he never mentions a Southern writer: "If allegory no longer receives any serious acceptance, it is because there is no longer any real need for it . . . Allegory, essentially a literary form that supports subjective qualities, cannot be expected to thrive when intellectual objective qualities dominate, as in

---

[40]Northrop Frye, *Anatomy of Criticism* (Princeton NJ: Princeton University Press, 1957) 90.

[41]Ibid., 89.

[42]Clifford, *The Transformations of Allegory*, 12.

[43]Gay Clifford supports the view that modern allegories have changed a great deal from books such as *Pilgrim's Progress*. In *Transformations of Allegory*, she writes, "Modern allegories differ from their predecessors in that there is no firmly established hierarchy of value to define or give meaning to the progress of the characters" (116). Process, the linear movement toward resolution, is frustrated at every turn. Allegory, Clifford adds, has gone underground: "From being the advocate of conventional social values, or at least of a conservative kind of wisdom, it tends to become subversive, satirical, and concerned with the predicament of the rebel and the outsider" (115-16).

neoclassical or contemporary society."[44] He then writes that with "few notable exceptions" allegory cannot find "really adequate bases of inspiration when ecumenical values are objective, realistic, and material—as they are at present —rather than subjective and inward-looking."[45] Yet the South described by O'Connor, McCullers, and Faulkner is, if nothing else, subjective and inward-looking. Its agonizing self-evaluation has brought it back to Scripture, to a religious-philosophical realm with few comforts. Assured of their sin, the major Southern characters described in this study seek a religious savior. Failing that, they turn to secular saviors in their fictional worlds.

2. Jesus as Allegorical Personage

No one is without Christianity, if we agree on what we mean by the word. It is every individual's individual code of behavior by means of which he makes himself a better human being than his nature wants to be. . . . Whatever its symbol—cross or crescent or whatever—that symbol is man's reminder of his duty inside the human race. Its various allegories are the charts against which he measures himself and learns to know what he is. . . . Writers have always drawn, and always will, from allegories of moral consciousness, for the reason that the allegories are matchless.[46]

—William Faulkner
From the "Art of Fiction" Series

Little—including ownership of land, reverence for family ties, and suspicion of strangers and "new-fangled contraptions"—could be said to be more important to Southern culture than its fundamentalist Protestant faith. With its tent revivals and born-again Christians, the South has absorbed a knowledge of the Bible and the stories of Christ that defies comparison. The transmitted Calvinistic belief system was an allegory of life—a war waged between Good and Evil in the presence of the Son of God, himself an allegory of God the

---

[44]Bloom, "The Allegorical Principle," 189.

[45]Ibid., 190.

[46]William Faulkner, quoted in "The Art of Fiction," *Paris Review* 12 (Spring 1956): 42.

Father. While William Faulkner, Carson McCullers, and other Southern writers would hardly call themselves Christian, they know at least the Calvinistic elements of Protestantism as well as they know the red clay of Georgia, the bayous of Louisiana, and the riverfront shanties of Mississippi. Standing jokes concerning Methodists and Baptists—stationed in churches on every corner—are common. Even a Georgia Catholic, Flannery O'Connor, chose to create Bible-thumpers and spirit-filled Protestants as she sought to enlarge her readers' conception of God. The Calvinist God of judgment, fire-and-brimstone damnation, and the concept of humankind as sinful creatures are alive and well.

These realities have created a theological mixed reaction in the South. While believing they are one step away from eternal damnation because of an account of a snake and an apple, Southerners also have their eyes turned inward. Seeking a reason for evil—assured of a mystical salvation of which they may avail themselves—the field is ripe for allegory. If life itself is a battle between the forces in one's soul, then a savior with blue eyes and sandy hair—dressed in a white toga to guarantee purity—is a ready conceptualization of a champion. Yet the Southern writer's familiarity with Christian myth does not simplify his or her metaphysical quest, nor does the myth necessarily appear in literature "as is." When it does, it often fails. For some, a surprising omission in this study is Faulkner's *A Fable*, described by F. W. Dillistone as a "narrative which keeps step with the journey from Galilee to Jerusalem though, in point of fact, the setting is the France of the later part of the 1914–18 war."[47] "No author," writes Ursula Brumm, "has invoked the shadow of Christ more often, covertly and openly, than William Faulkner."[48]

Yet *A Fable* is not set in the South, making it less appropriate for this study, and—more importantly—it invokes the figure of Christ far too openly. The novel is tedious and overly dramatic, a failure when compared with *Light in August* and *Go Down, Moses*, not—as Theodore Ziolkowski would suggest— because it is allegory, but because it is bad allegory. Recreating too directly the life of Christ and his twelve disciples, its drama is cloying—not nearly as powerful as the real thing. Ziolkowski asserts that the New Testament parallels are so "highly contrived and the psychological motivation so implausibly weak

---

[47]F. W. Dillistone, *The Novelist and the Passion Story* (New York: Sheed and Word, 1960) 94.
    [48]Brumm, *American Thought*, 207.

that one would suspect, were the book the least bit playful in spirit, that Faulkner is parodying himself."[49] Calling *A Fable* a "clumsy allegorical work,"[50] Ziolkowski dismisses allegory. An old general oversees the death of his son (who is thirty-three), and the novel ends with the funeral of the Supreme Commander. Ziolkowski interprets: "[A]fter the demise of Christianity, man is now confronted with the death of God."[51] Dillistone calls *A Fable* the "most ambitious attempt by any contemporary novelist to bring the Christian myth or allegory or history . . . into the very texture of the life of twentieth-century man."[52] It may be, but Faulkner has proven that the attempt is not enough.

Images of Christ far more successful than Faulkner's attempt in *A Fable* appear in non-Southern literature: *The Man Who Died* by D. H. Lawrence, *Brand* by Henrik Ibsen, and *The Confidence-Man* by Herman Melville. While little purpose is served by delving too deeply into these texts, it is necessary to note what makes them successful and to question why Southern writers continue to write Christian, allegorical literature, an anomaly in a century that is fundamentally secular. The Southern Renascence of the early half of the century features a Christian literature that has inherited its theology via Puritanism and Calvinism, its view of human nature from the Bible and the anti-Transcendentalists, and its natural expression of both from allegory. Although an allegory of Christ may be an oddity for Lawrence, Ibsen, or Melville, it is the rule in Southern fiction, a fiction that remains prevailingly religious.

In *The Man Who Died*, Lawrence adopts the parable style of "The Rocking-Horse Winner" ("There was a woman who was beautiful, who started with all the advantages, yet she had no luck . . . There were a boy and two little girls."[53]), adding geographic detail to style in *The Man Who Died*: "There was a peasant near Jerusalem who acquired a young gamecock which looked a shabby little thing."[54] References to Christ abound, but the man described is a modern rendition of the New Testament savior—the allegory parodies the

---

[49]Theodore Ziolkowski, *Fictional Transfigurations of Jesus* (Princeton NJ: Princeton University Press, 1972) 170-71.

[50]Ibid., 179.

[51]Ibid., 178.

[52]Dillistone, *The Novelist and the Passion Story*, 95.

[53]"The Rocking-Horse Winner," *The Norton Anthology of Short Fiction*, ed. R. V. Cassill (New York: W. W. Norton and Co., 1978) 788.

[54]D. H. Lawrence, *The Man Who Died* (New York: Random House, 1953) 163.

victory of Christ's death as told in the New Testament and sets up a sort of Albert Camus/Fyodor Dostoevsky existentialist hero. When the man awakes in a cave, the "bandages and linen and perfume fall away . . . He went on, on scarred feet, neither of this world or of the next . . . driven by a dim, deep nausea of disillusion."[55] The Messiah is dead; what is left is modern humanity. As he thinks of the "nails, the holes, the cruelty, the unjust cruelty against him who had offered only kindness,"[56] he leaves his message behind: "For men and women alike were mad with the egoist fear of their own nothingness. And he thought of his own mission, how he had tried to lay the compulsion of love on all men."[57] While the novel has many flaws, it is through the association of the qualities of Christ with a figure in literature that the allegory succeeds. It is, no doubt, modern allegory with a modern anti-hero, but while Lawrence's references to Jesus are no more subtle than Faulkner's, the inversion and irony save it from sentimentality.

Ibsen's *Brand* excels as allegory because of its subtle references to Jesus and its unobtrusive moral. (The conclusion, in which a voice thunders from the clouds crying, "He is the God of Love,"[58] is painfully overdramatized, but the play avoids other pitfalls of "the-moral-at-the-end.") The cultural criticism runs strong. Brand tells his followers,

> Your prayers
> Have not the strength nor the agony to reach
> To Heaven—except to cry:
> "Give us this day our daily bread!" That
> Is now the watchword of this country, the
>   remnant
> Of its faith.[59]

As his unwilling disciples follow him through danger to the Ice Church, Brand cries:

---

[55]Ibid., 166-67.
[56]Ibid., 204.
[57]Ibid., 184.
[58]Henrik Ibsen, *Brand* (New York: Doubleday and Co., 1960)157.
[59]Ibid., 65.

How long will you have to fight? Until you
    die!
What will it cost? Everything you hold dear.
Your reward? A new will, cleansed and strong.
A new faith, integrity of spirit;
A crown of thorns.[60]

Discovering the supremacy of love over missionary zeal, Brand learns grief and humility as his son dies. He learns to weep, and the doctor tells him, "I find you bigger now with your wings clipped/Than when you were the Angel of God."[61] Here the love and tenderness of Christ are revealed without over-emphasizing him, and the lesson is achieved without a pedantic preachiness.

Lambasted for its episodic, drifting structure, *The Confidence-Man* remains probably one of Melville's most powerful allegories and certainly the one that relies most heavily on the story of Christ. Ironic references to Scripture, with Jesus starring as the true confidence-man, are pervasive but not stifling. Lawrance Thompson writes, "It is certainly obvious that Melville's entire leaning toward an exceptional form of figurative and symbolic and allegorical narrative owes much to his having been saturated in Biblical modes of expression."[62] Elizabeth Foster, who accomplished one of the most thorough studies of Melville's final novel, says the book is an exploration of the nature of God, a "jokester, perhaps malevolent, perhaps indifferent."[63] Ralph Waldo Emerson (as well as Henry David Thoreau, although critics disagree) was on Melville's mind as he cast Mark Winsome and his disciple, Egbert. The novel becomes a satirical slam against Emerson's philosophies of optimism, individualism, and self-reliance, as well as of a Christian's smugness and pride. In marginalia next to a reference to Emerson, Melville writes, "But what did Christ see? He saw what made him weep—To annihilate all this nonsense read the Sermon on the Mount, and consider what it means."[64] While not

---

[60]Ibid., 145.

[61]Ibid., 103.

[62]Lawrance Thompson, *Melville's Quarrel with God* (Princeton NJ: Princeton University Press, 1952) 457.

[63]Elizabeth S. Foster, ed., *The Confidence-Man: His Masquerade*, by Herman Melville (New York: Hendricks House, 1954) xv.

[64]Quoted by Foster, ibid., lxxxi. (The word *implies* is substituted for *means* in the quotation cited in the text in a few of the Foster editions.)

ridiculing Christ the man, Melville does not take the common Symbol of Christianity and shows Christ's many faces. Certainly, he reveals the extinction of Christianity as the Fidéle's final light is extinguished.

Where Foster fails is in her comparison of *The Confidence-Man* to *Moby-Dick*, for her assessment relies on a judgment of literary forms and not the texts themselves. "*Moby-Dick* is greater," she writes, "because epic and tragedy are higher regions than allegory and satire. But within its domain, the art of *The Confidence-Man* is unique, and finished."[65] Thompson, however, lauds the novel for its "oblique allegorical artistry" and takes special pleasure in its attack on Thomas Carlyle's *Heroes and Hero-Worship*, as a "Great Man" is created to take "bitter sport" with others.[66]

Melville's microcosm sets sail with its cargo of pilgrims on April Fool's Day. The anti-hero of Melville's picaresque tale is a confidence-man, who dupes those around him in the process of revealing their hypocrisy and lack of trust in God and each other. R. W. B. Lewis moves to the heart of the debate concerning whether the confidence-man is Jesus or Satan by writing, "[Melville] only makes it clear that the Confidence Man is not the bringer of darkness; he is the one who reveals the darkness in ourselves. Whether this is the act of a devil or an angel may not, when all is said and done, really matter."[67]

The questions Melville raises in this depiction of a Christ figure of sorts are shattering ones: Are we able to know anything? Can we ever separate appearance from reality? Do we live in a world "thronging with impostors and masqueraders"?[68] From the mute in his cream-colored suit, to the man with a weed, to the herb doctor, to the Cosmopolitan, the eight faces of Christ that emerge serve Melville's satirical allegory well. (Turning the tables on his own allegory, Melville has the confidence-man speak the following: "Ah, now . . . irony is so unjust; never could abide irony; something Satanic about irony. God defend me from Irony, and Satire, his bosom friend."[69]) No one can be dissuaded by Melville's brief lapses into humor, for he knows that the cost of falling victim to the confidence-man is one's own soul. Having received

---

[65]Ibid., xcv.

[66]Thompson, *Melville's Quarrel*, 298-99.

[67]R. W. B. Lewis, "Afterword," in *The Confidence-Man*, by Herman Melville (New York: The New American Library, 1964) 276.

[68]Ibid., 263.

[69]Melville, *The Confidence-Man*, 144.

assurance from an old man that he trusts in Providence and that it protects him, the Cosmopolitan replies, " 'Be sure it will,' eyeing the old man with sympathy, as for the moment he stood, money-belt in hand, and life-preserver under arm, 'be sure it will, sir, since in Providence, as in man, you and I equally put trust.' "[70] Alluding to the Messiah who was often called the "Light of the World," Melville writes his final scene: "The next moment, the waning light expired, and with it the waning flames of the horned altar, and the waning halo round the robed man's brow; while in the darkness which ensued, the cosmopolitan kindly led the old man away."[71]

The Southern writer follows in the best tradition of allegory established by Melville and others, and references to Christ in American literature abound. While one might expect the South to be more concerned with history than fiction, its references to Jesus are not for the most part typological but allegorical. Jesus is not recreated but alluded to—a character may be Christ-like, but that connection is often immediately undercut, as it was in *The Man Who Died* and *The Confidence-Man*. For example, Faulkner's Joe Christmas—though his name might remind one of Jesus—is no innocent, as we shall explore. Abraham and Isaac, seen as types (or "figuras") of God and Christ, can be set up as historical parallels. But the John Singer, Haze Motes, Joe Christmas, Isaac McCaslin, and Gavin Stevens we shall meet are fictional —not copies of Christ but conglomerations in different degrees of the qualities Christ exhibited. All are failed messiahs. Neither Christ nor his characteristics are embodied in a Gandhi or a Martin Luther King in Southern literature; rejecting a historical parallel or typology (which is strange enough, considering the South's penchant for history), the Southern writer opts often for allegory, in which an image (Christian with his burden) is balanced by the idea (sin as a weight).

Some of the most famous images of Christ in modern Southern fiction include the "Gentleman Caller" of *The Glass Menagerie* (Tennessee Williams), who comes to Laura as a savior; the ironic Jesus who—at least in her mind— terrorizes Nancy, a servant of the Compsons in "That Evening Sun" (William Faulkner); the Misfit of "A Good Man Is Hard to Find" (Flannery O'Connor), an ironic Christ who shoots an elderly woman as she recognizes her kinship with all humanity; and Atticus of *To Kill a Mockingbird* (Harper Lee), a

---

[70]Ibid., 260.
[71]Ibid.

paragon of courage in Maycomb, Alabama, who is "civilized in his heart."[72] One of the most evocative portrayals of Jesus in fiction is the Jesus ironically omitted from O'Connor's "The Displaced Person." In it, a peacock (a medieval symbol of Christ) becomes the focal point for a selfish and vain Mrs. McIntyre and her priest. Jesus is not present as a character in the tale; in fact, it is Mr. Guizac, a homeless Polish man, who earns the story its title. Nonetheless, Jesus' very absence becomes conspicuous. It is important to note, however, that the priest and Mrs. McIntyre do not communicate; neither truly deals with the absent Christ, for the priest is soaring above reality and Mrs. McIntyre cannot see beyond it:

> The priest let his eyes wander towards the birds. They had reached the middle of the lawn. The cock stopped suddenly and curving his neck backwards, he raised his tail and spread it with a shimmering timbrous noise. Tiers of small pregnant suns floated in a green-gold haze over his head. The priest stood transfixed, his jaw slack. Mrs. McIntyre wondered where she had ever seen such an idiotic old man. "Christ will come like that!" he said in a loud gay voice and wiped his hand over his mouth and stood there gaping.
>
> Mrs. McIntyre's face assumed a set puritanical expression and she reddened. Christ in the conversation embarrassed her the way sex had her mother. "It is not my responsibility that Mr. Guizac has nowhere to go," she said. "I don't find myself responsible for all the extra people in the world."
>
> The old man didn't seem to hear her. His attention was fixed on the cock who was taking minute steps backward, his head against the spread tail. "The Transfiguration," he murmured.
>
> She had no idea what he was talking about. "Mr. Guizac didn't have to come here in the first place," she said, giving him a hard look.
>
> The cock lowered his tail and began to pick grass.
>
> "He didn't have to come in the first place," she repeated, emphasizing each word.

---

[72]Miss Maudie to Jem, in Harper Lee, *To Kill a Mockingbird* (New York: J. B. Lippincott Co., 1960) 107.

> The old man smiled absently. "He came to redeem us,"
> he said and blandly reached for her hand and shook it and said he
> must go.[73]

Though not an allegory, the story provides an outline and a symbol for Christ, the figure who determines the focus of so much of Southern literature. It may be that Christian allegory read only for its religious implications will have no more meaning for a reader than the peacock has for Mrs. McIntyre.

The Christ who drew the Southern writer was not the propagator of dogma but the merciful, suffering innocent who bound the common people. When Faulkner takes issue with Christianity, it is not Christ he mentions but the authoritarian church leaders who have stilled the bells of celebration in the belfries of the church. In a well-known interview with Jean Stein, Faulkner calls Jesus a "matchless example of suffering and sacrifice and the promise of hope."[74] W. H. Auden, in the preface of *Brand*, intensifies Faulkner's portrait of Christ the person:

> We still need to be constantly reminded that God's love and the
> mixture of sex, sentimentality, and mutual back-scratching which
> most human beings think of when they use the word "love" have
> nothing in common. We may call ourselves Christians, but our
> natural impulse on encountering the real Christ is to crucify Him
> because we find His love intolerable.[75]

The Southerner can only tell and retell the story of a Christlike figure in modern society through allegory. Robert Detweiler heralds allegory as "uniquely fitted for expression of the Christ figure." He writes, "[The nature of allegory] necessitates a treatment of a symbolic potential of Christ through attention to the biographical or doctrinal details of the Christ story, yet without implying commitment to the Christian faith."[76] Because allegory focuses on the "imaginative quality of the figure," it is "innocent of the

---

[73]Flannery O'Connor, *The Complete Stories* (New York: Farrar, Straus, & Giroux, 1973) 226.

[74]Faulkner, "The Art of Fiction," 42.

[75]W. H. Auden, "Preface," *Brand*, 40.

[76]Robert Detweiler, "Christ and the Christ Figure in American Fiction," *The Christian Scholar* 47 (1964) 118.

suspicion of 'remaking' Christ,"[77] he adds. Ursula Brumm agrees, identifying Christ as a figure "suited for use in literature" because he was needed more to "bear witness to man's divinity"[78] than to prove his own. According to Maureen Quilligan, Christianity also "shifted the locus of narrative conflict from external, historical events (Hector and Achilles . . .) to an internal, psychological place (Good versus Evil . . .)."[79] One might consider this a radical claim, but if true, Christianity fosters allegory, also a turning inward and a desire to represent with clarity the abstract characteristics and virtues that make us human. For these and other reasons, the South, grounded in and nourished by Christian doctrine, was primed for the explosion of allegorical fiction. However, one must not overlook that, for many writers, belief in a loving Christ died as Christianity itself floundered and fell. In a startling relation of the movement from Christianity to the skepticism of the modern world, Edwin Moseley writes of America,

> Like Gatsby, we are left in our silver armor with no illusions about the secret societies of the East, keeping our lonely vigil over Nothing. It is not far from this statement to a statement of no spiritual East, no Orient, no Rise after a Fall, no archetypal Christ as medicine man, healer, savior, regenerator, warmth-giving sun-god.[80]

The Southern writers in this study—if not their culture—have watched God beat a hasty retreat, but they cannot yet relinquish the vestiges of belief in a world ordained and directed by a merciful creator. One of the vestiges is Christ, and parting with him is a slow and wrenching process, as a reader learns in *The Heart Is a Lonely Hunter*, *Light in August*, and *Go Down, Moses*. If deliverance lies outside of Christ, where? The Southern writer clings to allegories of Christ and, in the process, renews the magic in the life of the Galilean.

---

[77]Ibid.

[78]Brumm, *American Thought and Religious Typology*, 206.

[79]Maureen Quilligan, *The Language of Allegory* (Ithaca NY: Cornell University Press, 1979) 285.

[80]Edwin Moseley, *Pseudonyms of Christ in the Modern Novel* (Pittsburgh: University of Pittsburgh, 1962) 133.

Carson McCullers

Photo courtesy Columbus College Archives, Chattahoochee Valley Historical Collections, Columbus, Georgia.
Printed with permission from John Zeigler, Charleston, South Carolina.

Chapter 3

Allegorical Representations of Christ

1. A Christ Made in Our Own Image

I have heard the mermaids singing, each to each.
I do not think that they will sing to me.

—T. S. Eliot
"The Love Song of J. Alfred Prufrock"

Although he knew many people in the town by name or face, the mute was his only
friend. They would idle in the quiet room and drink the ales. He would talk, and
the words created themselves from the dark mornings spent in the streets or in his
room alone. The words were formed and spoken with relief.

—Carson McCullers
The Heart Is a Lonely Hunter

About suffering they were never wrong,
The Old Masters: how well they understood
Its human position: how it takes place
While someone else is eating or opening a window or just walking dully along.

—W. H. Auden
"Musée des Beaux Arts"

"I've lost the presence of God!" cried the author of *The Heart Is a Lonely Hunter* late in her career. Remembered afterwards by the group of artists who had been with Carson McCullers at the Yaddo Artists Colony, the statement provides a pathetic thesis for both McCullers' life and her work. Haunted by a Christ who remained entombed, a twenty-one-year-old McCullers created an allegory in which numerous characters seek to work out their own salvation by relaying their individual fears to John Singer. Singer, a deaf mute, becomes a paralyzed Christ figure, so restricted by the expectations of others that he, too, must be considered a fiction. Only the author and the reader know Singer; Mick Kelly, Dr. Benedict M. Copeland, and Jake Blount merely fashion him into the savior they crave. For each he takes on a different face, a singular ministry. Copeland, a persecuted black doctor, believes Singer to be a Jew; Blount insists he's Irish. McCullers herself refers to Singer as a "repository," for all his friends "impute to him all the qualities which they would wish for him to have."[1] Furthermore, the all-too-ordinary theme of isolation in an indecipherable world attains heightened significance as each minor character in *The Heart Is a Lonely Hunter* embarks on his or her own spiritual quest. Each, says Margaret McDowell, is in "revolt against enforced isolation and his or her urge to express the self at all costs."[2] The novel is an allegory because of its dependence on the Christ figure, the individual quest, the significance of names, and the representative nature of each character. However, the novel is a *successful* allegory because Carson McCullers is not concerned with realism; she has constructed a consistent allegory in which theme is enriched by intricate symbolism.

While the perils of interpreting art via authorial experience or attitude must be evident by now, McCullers' own search for God can hardly be considered irrelevant to her first novel. In the early 1940s—with her husband Reeves gone, her relationship with David Diamond unresolved, and her professional standing in question—McCullers must have faced many of the same trials as her early characters. Virginia Spencer Carr, a McCullers biographer at Georgia State University, writes, "Above all, Carson felt that she needed God, that she must be able to pray again if she were to effect her own redemption."[3] In her book *The Lonely Hunter*, Carr writes, "McCullers recognized God as an omniscient being, a supreme creator who imposed order on the universe, but she sometimes saw Him as a capricious deity whose specialty

---

[1]Carson McCullers, "Author's Outline of 'The Mute' that is published as *The Heart Is a Lonely Hunter*," in *The Mortgaged Heart*, ed. Margarita G. Smith (Boston: Houghton Mifflin Company, 1971) 125.

[2]Margaret McDowell, *Carson McCullers* (Boston: Twayne Publishers, 1980) 31.

[3]Virginia Spencer Carr, *The Lonely Hunter* (New York: Doubleday and Company, 1975) 186.

was freaks."[4] Not only was McCullers alienated from God, she could not tap into the sense of place that sustained Eudora Welty, Flannery O'Connor, and William Faulkner. In an essay in *The Mortgaged Heart*, McCullers says, "A visit to Columbus in Georgia is a stirring up of love and antagonism."[5] While O'Connor reconciled herself to the Protestantism of the South and Faulkner claimed a love-hate relationship with his homeland, McCullers fled Georgia for New York. In a letter from Reeves to a friend, Reeves writes, "I have to keep Carson tied by a leg to the bedpost at times to keep her from going mad as she hates the South so."[6] In "How I Began to Write," McCullers says, "By that winter the family rooms, the whole town, seemed to pinch and cramp my adolescent heart. I longed for wanderings. I longed especially for New York. The firelight on the walnut folding doors would sadden me, and the tedious sound of the old swan clock."[7]

The Heart Is a Lonely Hunter was her only novel written in the South, and it was completed in Charlotte. One critic notes that McCullers "wanted nothing to do with the land of yokels and reactionaries."[8] Yet perhaps this perspective is too pat, for McCullers also said that the South provided a "truer pitch"; "When I work from within a different locale from the South, I have to wonder what time the flowers are in bloom—and what flowers? I hardly let characters speak unless they are Southern."[9] However, with animosity toward God and at least some toward country, it is small wonder that the fictional world of McCullers is peopled with those who long for a home. Yet while denying her Southern heritage, McCullers espoused a vision of the grotesque, as well as a theme of guilt and displacement, common to many of her Southern literary contemporaries. Hers is a strange rebellion; as Nathaniel Hawthorne said of Herman Melville,[10] she longed to believe and was unsettled in her

---

[4]Ibid., 194.

[5]McCullers, "The Flowering Dream: Notes on Writing," 279.

[6]Quoted from a letter to Vincent Adams, in Richard M. Cook, *Carson McCullers* (New York: Frederick Ungar Publishing Co., 1975) 9.

[7]McCullers, "How I Began to Write," in *The Mortgaged Heart*, 251.

[8]D. E. Presley, "Carson McCullers and the South," *The Georgia Review* 28 (Spring 1974): 26.

[9]McCullers, "The Flowering Dream: Notes on Writing," in *The Mortgaged Heart*, 279.

[10]In an entry dated 20 November 1856, Hawthorne wrote of Melville, "He can neither believe, nor be comfortable in his unbelief; and he is too honest and

unbelief. Ultimately, Heaven could offer no more solace than Columbus, Georgia, had.

McCullers' life reflects both deep pain and great courage, as she battled illness and social restrictions. Born in Columbus on 19 February 1917, McCullers suffered her first stroke in 1941 in Georgia. In 1947, at the age of thirty, she suffered two more strokes while in Paris; after these her left side was paralyzed, and the lateral vision in one eye was destroyed. Her biographers record that she was then unable to play the piano, type, or even turn pages. She did learn to walk with a cane after many months of therapy, but she eventually lost the ability to sign her name when the muscles in her hand and arm atrophied. In her short life, the writer had two operations to set and reset a fractured hip, four heart operations to prevent further strokes, and a mastectomy when cancer struck in 1962. Her death in 1967 was the result of a cerebral hemorrhage.

But McCullers suffered more than physical pain. At the age of twenty-four, she divorced Reeves and remarried him four years later. When she was thirty-six, she was planning a second divorce from him when he committed suicide in France. Both she and her husband were heavy drinkers; both, bisexual. McCullers fell in love with Annemarie Clarac-Schwarzenbach, a free-lance Swiss writer who was a friend of the Thomas Mann family. She was already married and in love with another woman; her death in 1942 affected McCullers profoundly. *Reflections in a Golden Eye*, McCullers' second novel, is dedicated to her. *The Ballad of the Sad Cafe* is dedicated to Diamond, with whom McCullers and her husband were in love. Diamond, a composer and violinist, met Reeves and his wife in 1941 and declared his love for both of them. Richard M. Cook attributes much of McCullers' emotional turmoil to a "perennial restlessness" and a "need for new and exotic relationships."[11] McDowell says, "A factor that may have contributed to her confused social and sexual life was her talent for making remarkably close friendships very quickly. Her open and direct manner shocked some and greatly attracted others."[12] Whatever the case, McCullers certainly lived a life characterized by confusion and pain and, to the end, longed for the something more she could never define.

---

courageous not to try to do one or the other." Cited in *The English Notebooks*, ed. Randall Stewart (New York: Russell & Russell, Inc., 1969) 433.

[11]Cook, *Carson McCullers*, 2.

[12]McDowell, *Carson McCullers*, 23.

The protagonist of McCullers' allegory of human noncommunication is John Singer. D. E. Presley explains the confessions of Jake Blount and Dr. Copeland by claiming they were "victims of a cruel joke." The mute, Presley believes, "does not understand a single word they say. Singer is like a dead god; those who trust in him, who believe in the redemptive potential of communication, deceive themselves."[13] Although Presley is correct in her assessment of the futility of human communication in this worst of all possible worlds, Singer cannot be considered ignorant of the messages directed his way. We are told early in the novel that he is a proficient lip reader. Neither is he a "dead god." It is his compassion—his interest in his fellows—that radiates from him. Accosted by strangers on the street, Singer cannot save his world, but he refuses to ignore it. "By midsummer," McCullers writes, "Singer had visitors more often than any other person in the house."[14] Late in the novel, Biff, proprietor of another sad café, wonders silently about the "dark guilt in all men, unreckoned and without a name" (199).

The individual fears and failings of Mick, Jake, and Copeland thereby assume symbolic significance. McCullers alludes to the Gospels in the following, with one important exception:

> Often it happened now that [Singer] would be spoken to and stopped during these walks. All kinds of people became acquainted with him. . . . His gray eyes seemed to take in everything around him, and in his face there was still the look of peace that is seen most often in those who are very wise or very sorrowful. He was always glad to stop with anyone wishing his company. For after all he was only walking and going nowhere (169-70).

This most reluctant of all messiahs has no destination, no sense of mission. Jesus, certainly, considered himself a living signpost to the kingdom of God. Singer simply wants companionship (as the reader learns while viewing Singer's relationship with Antonapoulos); he listens because others insist on seeking him out. McCullers writes of Singer, "His many-tinted gentle eyes were grave as a sorcerer's. Mick Kelly and Jake Blount and Doctor Copeland would come and talk in the silent room—for they felt that the mute would

---

[13]Presley, "Carson McCullers and the South," 28.

[14]McCullers, *The Heart Is a Lonely Hunter* (New York: Houghton Mifflin, 1977) 77. Subsequent references to this work will be cited in the text.

always understand whatever they wanted to say to him. And maybe even more than that" (81). Others interpret the quiet spirit of confidence and self-control, which Singer assuredly exhibits, as being all-knowing. Singer's very humanity is betrayed when those who have the potential to befriend him—to hear his song—create a messiah in their own image and begin to exploit him. McCullers promotes the reader's understanding through the eyes of Biff: "How Singer had been before was not important," he thinks. "The thing that mattered was the way Blount and Mick made him a sort of homemade God" (198). Through a sporadic omniscient point of view, the reader is told, "Each man described the mute as he wished him to be" (190). By making Singer divine, the townspeople depersonalize and, in effect, murder him.

The loneliest hunter of them all is John Singer. The reader meets the mute in the company of Antonapoulos, an obese deaf mute, who depends on Singer but also listens to him. Antonapoulos eventually is committed to a sanitarium, and Singer then writes letters he never mails—the opening, "My Only Friend," reminds the reader of how few have reached out to Singer. McCullers describes Singer after his loss: "This was the friend to whom he told all that was in his heart. . . . This was the Antonapoulos who now was always in his thoughts. . . . For something had happened in this year. He had been left in an alien land. Alone" (173). McCullers tells us that within Singer "there was always the memory of his friend. At night when he closed his eyes the Greek's face was there in the darkness. . . . In his dreams they were always together" (170). Singer writes to Antonapoulos that he "is not meant to be alone and without you who understand" (185). Yet even Antonapoulos fails him. During Singer's first visit to his absent friend, Antonapoulos becomes distracted when Singer's new friends surface in the conversation:

> He told Antonapoulos that they were strange people and always talking—but that he liked to have them come. He drew quick sketches of Jake Blount and Mick and Doctor Copeland. Then as soon as he saw that Antonapoulos was not interested, Singer crumpled the sketches and forgot about them. When the attendant came in to say that their time was up, Singer had not finished half of the things he wanted to say (80).

Singer, perhaps because he knows the pain of what remains unspoken, never fails to hear the words of the lost ones around him: "Singer nodded and wiped his mouth with his napkin. His dinner had got cold because he couldn't look down to eat, but he was so polite that he let Blount go on talking" (111).

Dependable and kind, Singer "was always the same to everyone," writes McCullers. "He sat in a straight chair by the window with his hands stuffed tight into his pockets, and nodded or smiled to show his guests that he understood" (78-79). The parallels between Singer and Christ in McCullers' allegory begin to be obvious—sometimes McCullers and sometimes Copeland point out the Jewishness of the mute: Singer "listened, and in his face there was something gentle and Jewish, the knowledge of one who belongs to a race that is oppressed" (114). Here is the man who is purported to have healed the sick, held children in his lap, and told parables to the uneducated and the poor. The description of Singer's visiting a hospital ward with Dr. Copeland easily reminds one of Christ's walking among the crowds of the sick and dying in Palestine:

> [Copeland] treated a syphilitic child and pointed out to Mr. Singer the scaling eruption on the palms of the hand, the dull, opaque surface of the eye, the sloping upper front incisors. . . . In a room where the fire burned low and orange on the hearth they were helpless while an old man strangled with pneumonia. Mr. Singer walked behind him and watched and understood. He gave nickels to the children (114-15).

The sensitivity, the gentleness, the love of children exhibited in such scenes set Singer apart from his fellows. While admired and respected, he becomes a kind of E. A. Robinson figure, crushed beneath the relentless weight of isolation and expectation like Richard Cory.

The pattern Singer follows as he moves unwittingly in and out of the lives of those about him establishes itself with Copeland, Mick, and Blount. A need to say, to articulate his need, binds them; stage two involves Singer, as he is thrust into the role of wise comforter; stage three is the realization of an emerging self; and stage four, a sense of betrayal and a renewed despair. Copeland, a healer of men's bodies, seeks also to save their souls for a higher good. Cook characterizes Copeland accurately as a man possessing a "selfless dedication that is as heroic as it is desperate."[15] When Copeland preaches—reaching a frenzy of political revival—a member of his audience cries, "Hallelujah! Save us, Lord!" The self-confident, powerful Copeland is revealed through his response: "Attention! We will save ourselves. Not by submission

---

[15]Cook, *Carson McCullers*, 32.

and humbleness. But by pride. By dignity. By becoming hard and strong" (165).

   While—unlike O'Connor—McCullers can hardly be considered a Christian writer, she doubtlessly is here pointing out the emptiness of self-reliance. It is Portia who sees her father's failures, and who reminds Copeland that a person's strength can only be partially self-generated. She, too, is the one who forces him to recognize the rift between his need and his heart. "You think out everthing [sic] in your brain," she says. "While us rather talk from something in our hearts that has been there for a long time" (67). Jesus, called the "Light of the World," takes ironic shape in Singer, who provides direction for Copeland. Once again, it is Portia who reveals Copeland's hidden fears—in a New Testament allegory of light and dark. "You haves grand electric lights," she states. "It don't seem natural why you all the time sitting in the dark like this." Copeland replies, simply and powerfully, "The dark suits me" (61). Here the reader must confront one of the many "messages" of McCullers' allegory.

   Copeland believes Singer is a Jew; he longs for identification with the members of oppressed races and cannot justify a friendship with a white man without casting him as a Jew. Singer appears in the doorway at one of Copeland's parties, as people turn to stare. Copeland describes him: "The mute stood by himself. His face resembles somewhat a picture of Spinoza. A Jewish face. It was good to see him" (159). Alone one night, Copeland remembers Singer and strangles on self-expression. Thoughts of Singer flow over him like a balm: "Doctor Copeland held his head in his hands and from his throat there came the strange sound like a kind of singing moan. He remembered the white man's face when he smiled behind the yellow match flame on that rainy night—and peace was in him" (77). Later in the tale, Copeland makes a visit to Singer's room and experiences the same kind of restoration: "He made half a dozen calls, and in the middle of the morning he went to Mr. Singer's room. The visit blunted the feeling of loneliness in him so that when he said goodbye he was at peace with himself once more" (126). The effect Singer has on the tuberculosis-ridden Copeland verges on the supernatural, the magic, the mysterious: "But with this tall, thin white man with the gray-green eyes something had happened that had never happened to him with any white man before" (73). Yet what Copeland cannot see is that the purveyor of peace, of sanity, is not peace itself. Singer, too, needs others and must strangle in loneliness without a confessor. When Singer commits suicide, an aging Copeland travels full circle and once again needs to speak: "The words in his heart grew big and they would not be silent. . . . there was no one to hear them" (287). Copeland has used Singer, but he has not learned from him; he doesn't know the mute, nor has he heard his story. Copeland is destined to live out his days embittered and alone, looking for strength within himself and questioning the death of his would-be savior.

Mick Kelly, too, recreates Singer, fantasizing about him and wondering about his death. McDowell could not be more in error when she suggests that Mick might be more important to the novel than Singer, that both Mick and Portia "reach out with some hope to the future."[16] McCullers admits to having organized the book in spokes that revolve around Singer. The novel itself is the story of "five isolated, lonely people in their search for expression and spiritual integration with something greater than themselves."[17] While an author is hardly always her own best critic, McCullers' words are easily supported. Although not the primary focus of the novel, Mick is an important figure, for she craves music and other expressions of the soul. Young Mick finds herself isolated by the very characteristics that bind her to Singer. Cook is correct when he recognizes that music for Mick "represents an ideal world of beauty and freedom beckoning beyond the confining limits of the everyday."[18] With little support from family and few friends at school, Mick internalizes the agonies of adolescence. Many critics have pointed out the parallels between the author of *The Heart Is a Lonely Hunter* and its young character. It is Mick who comes closest to recognizing her deification of Singer and who most closely echoes McCullers' own spiritual search: "Everybody in the past few years knew there wasn't any real God. When she thought of what she used to imagine was God she could only see Mister Singer with a long, white sheet around him. God was silent—" (101-102).

Here the reader faces the fallacy in the words of Presley, who sees only the unhearing, silent Singer. God is silent; Singer is not. Yet Singer never speaks. Where is McCullers pointing? Insistently, the author reminds us that understanding speaks louder than words, and the horror of the novel is that a deaf mute must show his fellows how to communicate. Soundlessly, Singer reaches out. Those with the physical means to speak are emotionally bankrupt; their words pour out unintelligibly. When Mick thinks of God, of salvation, she visualizes Singer. Yet Mick, too, is trapped. Presley claims that "Mick

---

[16]McDowell, *Carson McCullers*, 32.
[17]McCullers, "Author's Outline of 'The Mute,' " in *The Mortgaged Heart*, 125.
[18]Cook, *Carson McCullers*, 3.

Kelly's destiny as a clerk in Woolworth's is the author's projection of her future in the South, had she not escaped."[19] When Singer dies, Mick is as lost as Copeland or Blount: "Mick raked her hair from her forehead. Her mouth was open so that her cheeks seemed hollow. There were these two things she could never believe. That Mister Singer had killed himself and was dead. And that she was grown and had to work at Woolworth's" (300).

One story of despair blends into another. Jake is the only figure who speaks of his need in terms of Christ, but all cast Singer in the role of savior. Jake tells Singer about his early need for Jesus:

> My first belief was Jesus. There was this fellow working in the same shed with me. He had a tabernacle and preached every night. I went and listened and I got this faith. My mind was on Jesus all day long. In my spare time I studied the Bible and prayed. Then one night I took a hammer and laid my hand on the table. I was angry and I drove the nail all the way through. My hand was nailed to the table, and I looked at it and the fingers fluttered and turned blue (128).

This grotesque portrait is more in keeping with the fictional method of O'Connor, for here one finds the spiritual distortion of soul she often revealed. Jake threw himself into the arms of fundamentalist Christianity—with its tent revivals, wailing soloists, and damnation sermons. The Jesus he met demanded crucifixion, the annihilation of self. Haze Motes walks with stones and glass in his shoes; Hawthorne's Arthur Dimmesdale tortures himself in the privacy of his own dark soul. Guilt festers and spreads as humanity seeks release. Once again, it is the man's agonized spending of words that points to his poverty of soul: "Jake Blount leaned across the table and the words came out as though a dam inside him had broken" (20). Jake's outpouring also reinforces his identification with Christ: "The words swelled within him and gushed from his mouth . . . And at last the deluge of swollen words took shape and he delivered them to the mute with drunken emphasis: 'The things they have done to us! The truths they have turned into lies! The ideals they have fouled and made vile. Take Jesus. He was one of us. He knew' " (133-34). Biff, as always, provides the commentary on Jake's need to pour out his pain in language: Because it is in some people to "give up everything personal at some

---

[19]Presley, "Carson McCullers and the South," 20.

time, before it ferments and poisons—throw it to some human being or some human idea" (27). The man who must tell all—who seeks transformation in one who listens—cannot see beyond his own need to the loneliness of his priest.

The selflessness of Singer moves out and encompasses his fellows, making them long for the solace of his quiet spirit. The very room in which Singer sits communicates stillness, acceptance, peace. People come to him for renewal without heeding either their dependence or his personhood. They come face to face with the mute and meet themselves. Jake recalls Singer's giving spirit when Jake was taken home drunk. Jake "had got a lot of things off his chest and the man had listened," McCullers writes. "At first he would keep waking up with nightmares and have to turn the light on to get himself clear again. The light would wake this fellow also, but he hadn't complained at all" (46). Much of the power Singer possesses is entrusted to him by his fellows, who create characteristics in him to fill the void in themselves. "You're the only one in town who catches what I mean," says Blount. "For two days now I been talking to you in my mind because I know you understand the things I want to mean" (19). Singer, of course, may or may not understand any unarticulated message. But he has been endowed with the power to see, to understand, to heal.

In spite of our desire to create a heroic figure, one who can save us and unscramble the puzzle of our existence, the results are often only temporarily positive. By molding someone to reach out to us, we may learn to feel as we have not felt before. McCullers writes of Jake, "The mute's face was in his mind very clearly. It was like the face of a friend he had known for a long time . . . He began walking again down the hot, deserted street. He did not walk as a stranger in strange town" (52). Momentarily, Jake is placed, contained. His love for Singer knows no limits and explodes the bounds of reason. The ability to love so profoundly provides a restitution of its own, but because it is born of fantasy, such a love is short-lived. Not taking its object into consideration, love born in intense need is destined for disappointment. Just as Copeland's last thoughts are bitter, Blount's are full of despair. Singer is dead. A sense of betrayal infects the spirits of Copeland, Blount, and Mick. Finding himself once again drowning, Jake flees for the only solace he knows—the "mute's quiet room" (55).

McCullers writes, "In his confusion he had run all the way across the town to reach the room of his friend. And Singer was dead" (290). One may be reminded of the friends of Christ who gathered, grieving, at an empty tomb. His sancturary in ruins, Jake remembers "all the innermost thoughts that he had told to Singer, and with his death it seemed to him that they were lost" (291). Even in the throes of grief, Jake's thoughts are focused inward. The reader wonders: Why had Singer died? What was he lacking? Where was his foundation? The questions do not simply go unanswered; they go unasked. The receptacle of Jake's best self is dead. Copeland finds himself in total solitude; Jake stumbles through a darkened town in search of a dead messiah; and as a clerk in Woolworth's, Mick faces the end of her dreams.

McCullers' repetition and simplicity of style take their toll. Only occasionally are her analogies subtle, and too often she pummels the reader with Christ imagery. Yet her need to say is as profound as that of her characters, and she is capable of startling detail. In a rare moment of subtlety, McCullers has Alice, Biff's wife, teach a Sunday school class. Her text is the New Testament story of Simon and Andrew, who opt to follow Christ. Citing Mark 1:36-37, she reads, "And Simon and they that were with him followed after him. And when they had found him, they said unto him, 'All men seek for thee.' " All people seek for Christ, McCullers reminds us, no matter how they define him, no matter what they create him to be. What her earliest novel lacked in substance and form it made up in intensity and in understanding of the searchings of the heart. In *The Mortgaged Heart*, McCullers writes,

> Spiritual isolation is the basis of most of my themes . . . Love, and especially love of a person who is incapable of returning or receiving it, is at the heart of my selection of grotesque figures to write about—people whose physical incapacity is a symbol of their spiritual incapacity to love or receive love—their spiritual isolation.[20]

McCullers understands loneliness and the transience of life. When Biff loses Mick to adulthood, he remembers the effervescence, the hope of her childhood. His words could be the final message of each of the lives McCullers weaves: "And now, as a summer flower shatters in September, it was finished. There was no one" (305).

Deliverance from fear is but momentary. Biff does temporarily transcend the bondage of his fellows. Through an understanding of Singer's

---

[20]McCullers, "The Flowering Dream: Notes on Writing," in *The Mortgaged Heart*, 274.

life and death, Biff finds worth in human feeling. In an almost Faulkneresque tribute to human courage and emotion, McCullers writes of Biff, "For in a swift radiance of illumination he saw a glimpse of human struggle and of valor. Of the endless fluid passage of humanity through endless time. And of those who labor and of those who—one word—love" (306). Singer, Biff realizes, sacrificed himself in order to love. Swallowed by his own need, Singer is, of course, a flawed savior. He is not killed by religious leaders or Roman soldiers; as a modern man, he chooses to end his own life. Cook calls Singer, simply, the "embodiment of the community's need to find acceptance."[21] But through her portrayal of Singer and his disciples, McCullers accomplishes more than recreation of biblical myth. She has demonstrated the frailty of language, the ultimate failure of self-expression. As McCullers writes in an essay, "Communication is the only access to love—to love, to conscience, to nature, to God, and to the dream."[22] But, for all the peace and hope the characters of her first novel experience, each might as well be mute. As in modern life, McCullers' fictional universe contains too much need, too few listeners.

McDowell calls *The Heart Is a Lonely Hunter* McCuller's representation of her "regret that selfless love is rare and apt to be evanescent."[23] Faith is no option for secular mankind; men and women choose instead a flesh-and-blood hero to take the place of the prophet from Nazareth. When McCullers lists the themes she believes she has developed in the novel, a "unifying principle or God" plays a major role. "There is a deep need in man to express himself by creating some unifying principle or God," she writes in *The Mortgaged Heart*. "A personal God created by man is a reflection of himself and in substance this God is most often inferior to his creator." Another concept she supports fictionally is that in a "disorganized society these individual Gods or principles are likely to be chimerical and fantastic."[24] Because Copeland, Mick, and Blount create Singer to meet their needs, their god is not divine. He is all too human. Rather than his pointing the way to God through a Gethsemane moment, isolation damns Singer. His song is never heard.

---

[21]Cook, *Carson McCullers*, 38.

[22]McCullers, "The Flowering Dream: Notes on Writing," in *The Mortgaged Heart*, 281-82.

[23]McDowell, *Carson McCullers*, 15.

[24]McCullers, "Author's Outline of 'The Mute,'" in *The Mortgaged Heart*, 124.

McCullers has written an allegory of the human search for self, and the glimpses remain rare and incomplete. Whatever the stylistic failures of *The Heart Is a Lonely Hunter*, she has successfully explored what she termed the "solitary region of simple stories and the inward mind."[25] Her characters do not carry a pack labelled "Sin" on their backs, but Singer may easily be read as an allegorical Everyman. The pain of the characters is as internal as it is destructive, and their cries for deliverance go unheard.

2. *Wise Blood* and the "Ragged Figure" in the Mind

> *But as I rav'd and grew more fierce and wilde*
> *At every word,*
> *Me thought I heard one calling, Child!*
> *And I reply'd, My Lord.*

—George Herbert
"The Collar"

> *I fled Him, down the nights and down the days;*
> *I fled Him, down the arches of the years,*
> *I fled Him, down the labyrinthine ways*
> *Of my own mind.*

—Francis Thompson
"The Hound of Heaven"

> *. . . me frantic to avoid thee and flee . . .*
> *the hero whose heaven-handling flung me, foot trod*
> *Me? or me that fought Him? O which one? is*
> *it each one? That night, that year*
> *of now done darkness I wretch lay wrestling*
> *with (my God!) my God.*

—Gerard Manley Hopkins
"Carrion Comfort"

---

[25]McCullers, "How I Began to Write," 251.

Flannery O'Connor took issue with a world in which Jesus was but another moral man, in which the Incarnation was valid only to the unintellectual, and in which people could—through their own actions or natural goodness—save themselves. In O'Connor, one can most easily understand the modernist's contention that allegory is too innately didactic to be taken seriously as art. Yet, while her allegory is undeniably didactic, her characters remain representative. It is ironically *because* O'Connor chose to write allegory that her work is defensible: blindness, denial, violence, and grace, for example, take on strong New Testament overtones, but all function as easily on other levels. O'Connor pleaded guilty to dogmatism, but her unique defense in a letter of August 2, 1955, is notable: "Dogma can in no way limit a limitless god. . . . For me a dogma is only a gateway to contemplation and is an instrument of freedom and not of restriction."[26] Christianity gave O'Connor a system—a method for seeing—which she denied ever obstructed or clouded her view. Her faith, humor, and her fearless self-expression set her apart from a culture ambivalent or hostile to her central focus. "One of the awful things about writing when you are a Christian," she said, "is that for you the ultimate reality is the Incarnation, the present reality is the Incarnation, and nobody believes in the Incarnation."[27]

O'Connor minced neither words nor beliefs. Of Christ she said, "If He was not God, He was no realist, only a liar, and the crucifixion an act of justice."[28] Her determination to see truth as static and morals as unbendable dominates her first novel, *Wise Blood.* Haze Motes, who tries ineffectually throughout the novel to elude Christ, wakes in terror in his train berth and cries to the porter for help. "I'm sick!" he yells. "I can't be closed up in this thing. Get me out!" Standing and watching him, the porter states the message of O'Connor's world, "Jesus been a long time gone."[29]

To understand *Wise Blood* and tolerate its theological inflexibility, one must account for O'Connor's own religious vision, clarify the fundamentalist Protestant spirit central to her work, and delineate new directions for allegory. O'Connor takes the reader's incredulity for granted; Haze, too, is after all

---

[26] *The Habit of Being*, ed. Sally Fitzgerald (New York: Farrar, Straus, & Giroux, 1979) 92.

[27] Ibid.

[28] Ibid.

[29] Flannery O'Connor, *Wise Blood* (New York: New American Library, 1962) 19. Subsequent references to this work will be cited in the text.

living up to the implications of his first name as he denies Christ three times. By the third denial, the parallels with Simon Peter's threefold denial of his Lord are obvious. On the train in chapter one, Haze meets Mrs. Wally Bee Hitchcock, with her "poisonous Eastern voice." Ever the personable fellow, Haze glares at her and asks, "Do you think I believe in Jesus? . . . Well I wouldn't even if He existed. Even if He was on this train." Mrs. Hitchcock replies, "Who said you had to?" (13). Second, a taxi driver says to Haze in Taulkinham (probably Atlanta), "You look like a preacher. That hat looks like a preacher's hat. . . . It ain't only the hat. It's a look in your face somewheres [sic]." Haze retorts, "Listen. Get this: I don't believe in anything" (21). Finally, while in the home of Leora Watts, a prostitute, Haze says "in a voice that was higher than his usual voice," "What I mean to have you know is: I'm no goddam preacher" (23). Watts, of course, can't remember having asked if he were. The preacher Asa Hawks speaks of the "urge for Jesus" (31) in Haze's voice, but it is only after disillusionment, murder, and physical blindness that Haze confronts his own need. Haze, like the reader, O'Connor implies, is a doubter who may be avoiding the inevitable meeting with the incarnate Word. As she writes to Cecil Dawkins, deciding on a moral system to govern behavior is not enough.

> I don't really think the standard of judgment, the missing link, you spoke of that you find in my stories emerges from any religion but Christianity, because it concerns specifically Christ and the Incarnation, the fact that there has been a unique intervention in history. It's not a matter in these stories of Do Unto Others. That can be found in any ethical culture series. It is the fact of the Word made flesh.[30]

Just as Nathaniel Hawthorne's focus in "The Custom-House" was the moment when reality meets mystery, O'Connor's concern rivets to the moment when one's need to believe meets one's reason. In a letter dated September 13, 1959, O'Connor writes, "I don't think you should write something as long as a novel around anything that is not of the gravest concern to you and everyone else and for me this is always the conflict between an attraction for the Holy and the disbelief in it that we breathe in with the air of

---

[30]Fitzgerald, *The Habit of Being*, 226-27.

the times."[31] The same year she wrote, "I think there is no suffering greater than what is caused by the doubts of those who want to believe."[32] Certainly, Haze's own quest is largely a railing against belief, but in true New Testament form, his creator sees victory in his ultimate submission. In "On Her Own Work," an essay in *Mystery and Manners*, O'Connor writes,

> That belief in Christ is to some a matter of life and death has been a stumbling block for readers who would prefer to think it is a matter of no great consequence. For them, Hazel Motes' integrity lies in his trying with such vigor to get rid of the ragged figure who moves from tree to tree in the back of his mind. For the author, his integrity lies in his not being able to.[33]

O'Connor is sympathetic to the pain of *Wise Blood's* Enoch Emory, who seeks a friend; Onnie Jay Holy, who deludes himself into selling religion; and Haze, who longs for and repudiates Christ. She undoubtedly sees them as representatives of seekers in her own world, as the names she has chosen for them indicate. Gilbert Muller notes, "The absurd agonies of Miss O'Connor's characters present a penetrating critique of the purposelessness of existence without God."[34]

In O'Connor's fictional boundaries, a reader is not permitted to be satisfied with the individual system of order Ernest Hemingway advocates in works such as "A Clean, Well-Lighted Place," or with William Faulkner's admonition to endure and prevail. It is not enough to roam from café to café in hopes of solace and companionship, nor is there sufficient justification in Dilsey's love or Gail Hightower's eventual self-awareness. Men and women must acknowledge their need for God and come to Him in humility. As Louis Rubin argues, for O'Connor the "struggle against Satan is individual, continuous and desperate, and salvation is a personal problem, which comes not through ritual and sacrament, but in the gripping fervor of immediate

---

[31]Ibid., 349.

[32]Ibid., 353.

[33]Flannery O'Connor, "On Her Own Work," in *Mystery and Manners*, eds., Sally and Robert Fitzgerald (New York: Farrar, Straus, & Giroux, 1969) 114-15.

[34]Gilbert H. Muller, *Nightmares and Visions: Flannery O'Connor and the Catholic Grotesque* (Athens GA: University of Georgia Press, 1972) 112.

confrontation with eternity."[35] If O'Connor breaks with her Catholic heritage, it is here, for she sees in the Protestant frenzy of penance and revival the stuff of fiction. In fundamentalist Protestantism she finds her unworthy protagonist, whom Miles Orvell describes as a man of "presumably deformed emotions, seeking, in a world of failed human relationships, the lost God."[36] While Robert Milder and others argue the "paradox that this most aggressively Catholic of American writers should have produced a corpus so uncompromisingly Protestant in substance,"[37] it is the similarity between Catholic and Protestant doctrine that should draw our attention.

Three concepts—original sin, a mysterious God, and grace—are central to the faith of a Catholic and a Protestant. According to Milder, original sin for O'Connor is equivalent to the "self," and "before grace can be extended to a character, that 'self' must be annihilated."[38] The sinner must realize his or her helplessness; humiliation and pain trigger salvation. Because humanity is innately sinful, the state of faith does not serve as a barricade against reality; instead, it plunges humankind into the thick of conflict. True sight (understanding/awareness) comes only through death, mortification, and denial of self in O'Connor's world. Too many, O'Connor says, think "faith is a big electric blanket, when of course it is the cross."[39] In "Catholic Novelists," O'Connor again reminds the reader that faith is a "walking in darkness" and not a "theological solution to mystery."[40] Because human beings fail and their salvation involves Søren Kierkegaard's step into the unknown, pride once again becomes the most unpardonable of sins. Milder writes that if one evil lies at the root of all others in O'Connor's work, it is the "pride of secular intelligence, the arrogant and self-deluded belief that man can be his own savior."[41]

The notion of grace is bound up with the Calvinist doctrine of the omnipotent and angry God. Conversions in O'Connor's fiction occur in the

---

[35]Louis Rubin, "Flannery O'Connor and the Bible Belt," in *The Added Dimension*, ed. Melvin J. Friedman and Lewis A. Lawson (New York: Fordham University Press, 1977) 50.

[36]Miles Orvell, *Invisible Parade* (Philadelphia: Temple University Press, 1972) 68.

[37]Robert Milder, "The Protestantism of Flannery O'Connor," *The Southern Review* 11 (1975): 802.

[38]Ibid., 812-13.

[39]O'Connor, *The Habit of Being*, 354.

[40]O'Connor, "Catholic Novelists," in *Mystery*, 184.

[41]Milder, "The Protestantism of Flannery O'Connor," 807.

moment of violence, never in the company of angels. Milder states, "For Miss O'Connor, as for the Protestant, the foundation of religious life lay not in the Church or the sacraments, but in the private and often terrifying experience of divine grace."[42] Catholic critic Walter Sullivan, too, reminds us that God's mercy may be "terrible and sure."[43] No one escapes the need to be saved from one's own nature. God is just and merciful, yes, but His ways lie beyond our knowing. God always, Sullivan says, "gets His way in the end."[44] O'Connor remains interested in mental and spiritual deformity because she sees it as symptomatic of an age that has forgotten the cost of mercy: "Our age not only does not have a very sharp eye for the almost imperceptible intrusions of grace, it no longer has much feeling for the nature of the violences which precede and follow them."[45] Modern men and women do not work out their own salvation, believes O'Connor, because they have not yet come to terms either with their guilt or with the upheaval that must accompany their transformation.

In *History of Plymouth Plantation* William Bradford hopes that Roger Williams will be "[reduced] into the way of truth."[46] O'Connor's avenue to truth is at least as restrictive as the Pilgrim leader's. In a significant scene in *Wise Blood*, Haze kills Solace Layfield, a false prophet who functions as the embodiment of all that disgusts Haze in himself. His self-justification? "Two things I can't stand," Haze says, "a man that ain't true and one that mocks what is" (111). Here an unconverted Hazel Motes—the man who believes in nothing and preaches the Church Without Christ—acknowledges a higher truth that cannot be ridiculed with impunity. In a letter of March 17, 1956, O'Connor writes, "It is popular to believe that in order to see clearly one must believe in nothing. This may work well if you are observing cells under a microscope. It will not work if you are writing fiction. For the fiction writer, to believe nothing is to see nothing."[47]

O'Connor never apologized for her Christian theology, for her vision of Truth outstretching a man's or a woman's intellect. In "The Fiction Writer

---

[42]Ibid., 812.

[43]Walter Sullivan, *Death by Melancholy: Essays on Modern Southern Fiction* (Baton Rouge LA: Louisiana State University Press, 1972) 35.

[44]Ibid., 23.

[45]O'Connor, *Mystery*, 112.

[46]In *The Puritans*, eds., Perry Miller and Thomas J. Johnson (New York: Harper and Row, 1963) 1:111.

[47]O'Connor, *Habit of Being*, 147.

and His Country," she states, "I have heard it said that belief in Christian dogma is a hindrance to the writer, but I myself have found nothing further from the truth. Actually, it frees the storyteller to observe. It is not a set of rules which fixes what he sees in the world. It affects his writing primarily by guaranteeing his respect for mystery."[48] Again, in "Writing Short Stories," she says, "Your beliefs will be the light by which you see, but they will not be a substitute for seeing."[49] Her faith was not the faith of a Protestant fundamentalist, for she revered mystery and trusted the providence and mercy of God. She stared into the heart of metaphysical tensions and looked suffering and despair in the face. While Haze might have walked in spiritual fog, O'Connor accepted the wages of faith, knowing that one's discoveries might be startling. In a letter dated September 6, 1955, she writes,

> M. Sartre finds God emotionally unsatisfactory in the extreme, as do most of my friends of less stature than he. The truth does not change according to our ability to stomach it. A higher paradox confounds emotion as well as reason and there are long periods in the lives of all of us, and of the saints, when the truth as revealed by faith is hideous, emotionally disturbing, downright repulsive.[50]

O'Connor's theological notions form the foundation for her views concerning violence and the grotesque, two major components in her allegories. Once again, as in Ralph Waldo Emerson, Nathaniel Hawthorne, Herman Melville, and others, the visible universe suggests an invisible one. As Muller states, O'Connor "realized that only a stern intellect, an adamant faith, and an accretion of humor which usually shaded into the grotesque could confront suffering, violence, and evil in this world."[51] Two principles govern O'Connor's use of the grotesque: (1) her belief that humankind spirals toward eternity, and (2) the realization that, as a philosophical oddity, she would have to jolt a complacent reader into consciousness. In a powerful letter from the summer of 1955, O'Connor writes an acknowledgment that her stories are hard, "but they are hard because there is nothing harder or less sentimental than Christian realism." She writes, "I believe that there are many rough beasts

---

[48]O'Connor, "The Fiction Writer and His Country," in *Mystery*, 31.
[49]O'Connor, "Writing Short Stories," in *Mystery*, 91.
[50]O'Connor, *Habit of Being*, 100.
[51]Muller, *Nightmares and Visions*, 2.

now slouching toward Bethlehem to be born and that I have reported the progress of a few of them, and when I see these stories described as horror stories, I am always amused because the reviewer always has hold of the wrong horror."[52] In "The Fiction Writer and His Country," she adds further justification for her fictional method: "When you can assume that your audience holds the same beliefs you do, you can relax a little and use more normal means of talking to it; when you have to assume that it does not, then you have to make your vision apparent by shock—to the hard of hearing you shout, and for the almost-blind you draw large and startling figures."[53]

The grotesque character, defined by Sherwood Anderson in the well-known preface to *Winesburg, Ohio,* subverts all experience into a belief in one central Truth. Characters become grotesques through a failure to live the examined life; their vision distorts and makes them unable to communicate. Like Hawthorne, O'Connor is ever aware of the perils of isolation. Because, as O'Connor writes in *Mystery and Manners,* Christians may tap into the understanding and vision of the Most High, they have the potential to see more clearly than some of those around them: "My own feeling is that writers who see by the light of their Christian faith will have, in these times, the sharpest eyes for the grotesque, for the perverse, and for the unacceptable."[54] As Stuart Burns notes in his article, "Freaks in a Circus Tent," O'Connor's characters are often "anguished seekers" or "diabolic agents of grace."[55] Whoever they are, they are Christ-haunted. "Taken compositely," writes Burns, "they further the author's theme that true Christian grace is so rare a quality in contemporary society as to be viewed as abnormal or grotesque."[56] Because Christians often call on the wisdom of God in defining their world, O'Connor believed, they are uniquely capable of discerning the grotesque; they also are able to recognize their own separation from their fellows, a grotesque quality in themselves.

With the grotesque comes violence, for maladjusted individuals separated from their fellows are not likely to operate in modern society as redemptive forces. One "agent of grace," the Misfit in "A Good Man Is Hard

[52]O'Connor, *Habit of Being,* 90.
[53]O'Connor, "The Fiction Writer and His Country," in *Mystery,* 34.
[54]Ibid., 33.
[55]Stuart L. Burns, "Freaks in a Circus Tent: Flannery O'Connor's Christ-Haunted Characters," *The Flannery O'Connor Bulletin* 1 (Autumn 1972): 3.
[56]Ibid.

to Find," speaks of Christ as one who "thrown everything off balance and it's nothing for you to do but follow Him or find some meanness."[57] There is with O'Connor little question concerning the option the Misfit chooses. The grandmother in the tale is "saved," for when she stares into the barrel of the Misfit's gun, the priorities of life fall into place. The Misfit's pronouncement that the grandmother would have been a good woman if there had been someone there to shoot her every minute of her life points out the ironic necessity of violence as a means (and often an outgrowth) of salvation. Daniel F. Littlefield blames the grotesqueness of O'Connor's characters on the "distortion of spiritual purpose," itself a product of America's "unparalleled prosperity."[58] He is not wrong, but he is off the mark. C. Hugh Holman's assessment in "Her Rue with a Difference" is far more accurate. In a discussion of grotesque figures in Southern literature, he writes, "Living in a world not ordered to an adequate sense of the power and presence of God, they seek either to deny Him or to pervert Him, and thus they become grotesque and unnatural."[59] One example is Haze, who kills Layfield by running over him with his rat-colored car. The man, though lying in the dirt, is not yet dead. "You shut up now," Haze tells him. "Jesus," Layfield whispers. Haze tells him again, "Shut up like I told you to now." "Jesus hep me," the man says before Haze silences him for good. As if not horrifying enough, O'Connor records that the "bumper had a few splurts of blood on it but that was all" (111).

In the violence of the grotesque, O'Connor employs allegory. While far from the only Southern writer to do so, O'Connor stood in humble relation to writers such as Faulkner. In two letters written in 1958, O'Connor acknowledged her standing: "I keep clear of Faulkner so my own little boat won't get swamped" and "Probably the real reason I don't read [Faulkner] is because he makes me feel that with my one-cylinder syntax I should quit writing and raise chickens altogether."[60] Although she makes few comparisons between herself and other Southern writers, she was grounded in Hawthorne and Kafka.

One of the stories that best illustrates her affinity for parable is "The Lame Shall Enter First," in which an ironic Christ figure discovers the

---

[57]Cited in O'Connor, *Habit of Being*, 227.

[58]Daniel F. Littlefield, "Flannery O'Connor's *Wise Blood*: 'Unparalleled Prosperity' and Spiritual Chaos," *Mississippi Quarterly* 23 (Spring 1970): 23.

[59]C. Hugh Holman, "Her Rue with a Difference," in *The Added Dimension*, 86.

[60]O'Connor, *Habit of Being*, 273, 291-92.

limitations of good works. The protagonist's name is—not surprisingly—Sheppard. He and his son, Norton, take in a stray child, Rufus Johnson. When Norton tells Rufus that his father is "good. . . . He helps people," a partially crippled Rufus hisses, "Listen here. I don't care if he's good or not. He ain't right!"[61] Later, his goal becomes to "show up that big tin Jesus! He thinks he's God. . . . When I get ready to be saved, Jesus'll save me, not that lying stinking atheist."[62] The ironies in the tale converge when Sheppard, issuing a threat, says, "I'm stronger than you are and I'm going to save you. The good will triumph." Rufus replies, "Save yourself. Nobody can save me but Jesus."[63] Offended because Rufus was not grateful for a new shoe for his lame foot, Sheppard watched the police arrest Rufus for theft and says to himself, "Perhaps after a night in jail it would mean even more to the boy."[64] Inevitably, the moment of revelation—of conversion—occurs for Sheppard:

> His every action had been selfless, his one aim had been to save Johnson for some decent kind of service, he had not spared himself, he had sacrificed his reputation, he had done more for Johnson than he had done for his own child. . . . His heart constricted with a repulsion for himself so clear and intense that he gasped for breath. He had stuffed his own emptiness with good works like a glutton. He had ignored his own child to feed his vision of himself.[65]

"The Lame Shall Enter First" supports what Milder defines as the "Protestant [defined synonymously with Calvinistic and Puritan] doctrine of the absolute corruption of all good works not founded upon divine grace."[66] He states, "It is an uncompromising vision and, to the humanist, an appalling one."[67] In this tale—even more "realistic" than many of O'Connor's pieces—the characters take part in allegory. Rufus, the agent of grace, brings Sheppard

---

[61]Flannery O'Connor, "The Lame Shall Enter First," in *The Complete Stories* (New York: Farrar, Straus, & Giroux, 1973) 454.

[62]Ibid., 480.

[63]Ibid., 474.

[64]Ibid., 465.

[65]Ibid., 481.

[66]Milder, "The Protestantism of Flannery O'Connor," 808.

[67]Ibid.

to new realization. As O'Connor said in a letter of September 6, 1962, Sheppard represents an "empty man who fills up his emptiness with good works."[68] On a more complex level, Sheppard is a failed Christ, who sets out through his own powers to save the world. The result in O'Connor's world is obvious.

Carol Shloss writes that O'Connor wrote during a time when allegory had become impossible.[69] While this is admittedly an exaggeration, it is true that allegory had become difficult. While the spiritual import of her work is central, much of her fiction may be read as John R. May prescribes:

> Meaning in O'Connor's fiction like meaning in the parables of Jesus is accurately expressed only in terms of universal human experience. If their meaning is fundamentally religious, it is because they confront man with his radical poverty in the face of reality. They startle him with the suddenness of the sacred in the midst of the ordinary.[70]

The purpose of parable mirrors the purpose of O'Connor's work: to startle us into awareness. Allegory, as O'Connor employs it, is not a predictable system, although one may assume that an understanding of O'Connor's beliefs sets up one level of reading. What Orvell proposes unfortunately has emerged in the critical world as the minority voice: "What the book does legitimately demand is that it be read as one *image* of Christian reality. And images may represent a version of reality without demanding a belief in the image itself."[71] A belief in Christianity, while not necessary or inevitable, simplifies an understanding of the symbolic tensions within the text. Asked about the symbols in her work, O'Connor replied in 1954 with a familiar tongue-in-cheek line: "A symbol should go on deepening. Everything should have a wider significance—but I am a novelist not a critic and I can excuse myself from *explication de textes* on that ground. The real reason of course is laziness."[72]

---

[68]O'Connor, *The Habit of Being*, 491.

[69]Carol Shloss, *Flannery O'Connor's Dark Comedies* (Baton Rouge LA: Louisiana State University Press, 1980) 31.

[70]John R. May, *The Pruning Word: The Parables of Flannery O'Connor* (Notre Dame: University of Notre Dame Press, 1976) 13.

[71]Orvell, *Invisible Parade*, 92.

[72]O'Connor, *Habit of Being*, 70.

Besides contending with the restrictions of the Christian message and the reputation of allegory, O'Connor was confronted with the image problems of a "Southern writer." In an essay entitled "The Regional Writer," O'Connor characterizes her confrontation with American literature: "As far as I know, the heroes of Hawthorne and Melville and James and Crane and Hemingway were balanced on the Southern side by Br'er Rabbit—an animal who can always hold up his end of the stick, in equal company, but here too much was expected of him."[73] In the article, "Flannery O'Connor and the Bible Belt," Rubin graphically describes the Protestant monopoly on religion:

> All too frequently it is the kind of orgiastic, hyper-emotional religion that anyone who has ever lived in the South has heard preached on the numerous little low-wattage radio stations, interspersed with the Hillbilly Hit Parade. . . . It is the fanatical, intolerant, anti-intellectual; the God of the Old Testament and of the Book of Revelation is there, but the God of the Sermon on the Mount is seldom invoked.[74]

O'Connor, Rubin asserts, used the world in which the Pope is a "minion of Satan" and a priest a "mysterious and dangerous man" to produce allegory:

> The fanaticism and torment that characterize the emotion-torn, apocalyptic primitive Protestantism of the back country South, with its revivals, evangelists, testimonies, visions, prophets, and hallucinations, became in her fiction the unlettered, naive search for spiritual existence in a world grown complacent and materialistic.[75]

The fanatics she portrayed represented the Everyman in a quest for self. Milder, however, says O'Connor was setting up more than an allegorical system; while fearing the extremism of Protestantism, he says, she nonetheless felt what he terms "an almost involuntary admiration for the intensity of its faith":

---

[73]O'Connor, "The Regional Writer," in *Mystery*, 55.
[74]Rubin, "Flannery O'Connor and the Bible Belt," 70.
[75]Ibid., 53.

> Armed only with the Bible and his own invincible faith, the
> Fundamentalist went forward to a life of incessant battle against the
> temptations of the world. It was a strenuous but immensely
> exhilarating vision in which each moral decision became a contest
> between God and Satan and the smallest gesture assumed a
> profound anagogical significance.[76]

Milder is on the right track, for O'Connor herself said Protestant believers are
easier to write about than Catholics "because they express their belief in diverse
kinds of dramatic action which is obvious enough for me to catch."[77]

Unlike McCullers, O'Connor showed no animosity toward her
homeland and no bitterness about her lot in life or her illness. The fundamentalist roots of the South provided subject matter for her, since, as she said,
"While the South is hardly Christ-centered, it is most certainly Christ-
haunted."[78] She, like the Agrarians of Vanderbilt, mourned the loss of the
Southern values she believed were worth keeping, although she had not turned
the Deep South into a Camelot:

> The anguish that most of us have observed for some time now has
> been caused not by the fact that the South is alienated from the rest
> of the country, but by the fact that it is not alienated enough, that
> every day we are getting more and more like the rest of the country,
> that we are being forced out not only of our many sins, but of our
> few virtues.[79]

Ultimately, it is O'Connor's sense of reality and her enduring spirit that helped
her face both cultural deprivations and illness, a disease called lupus epizooticus
which made crutches necessary for the last nine years of her life. "The
advantages and disadvantages of being a Southern writer can be endlessly
debated," wrote O'Connor, "but the fact remains that if you are, you are."[80]
Her attitude toward pain revealed even more of her nature. In a letter of June
28, 1956, O'Connor wrote, "In a sense sickness is a place, more instructive
than a long trip to Europe, and it's always a place where there's no company,

---

[76]Milder, "The Protestantism of Flannery O'Connor," 818-19.
[77]O'Connor, *Habit of Being*, 517.
[78]O'Connor, *Mystery*, 44.
[79]Ibid., 28-29.
[80]O'Connor, *Habit of Being*. 230.

where nobody can follow."[81] Perhaps both attitudes were made possible through her faith, which—according to most critics—damaged her fiction and preserved her hope. In an essay entitled "The King of the Birds," O'Connor refers to the peacock, ancient symbol of Christ, in an avowal of the eternal joy offered his followers: "I intend to stand firm and let the peacocks multiply, for I am sure that, in the end, the last word will be theirs."[82]

O'Connor acknowledged repeatedly that her first novel could not have been written by someone with a different religious foundation. "Haze," she explained, "is saved by virtue of having wise blood; it's too wise for him ultimately to deny Christ."[83] In another letter she writes,

> Let me assure you that no one but a Catholic could have written *Wise Blood* even though it is a book about a kind of Protestant saint. It reduces Protestantism to the twin ultimate absurdities of The Church Without Christ or The Holy Church of Christ Without Christ, which no pious Protestant would do. And of course no unbeliever or agnostic could have written it because it is entirely Redemption-centered in thought.[84]

In addition to its message of salvation, *Wise Blood* also portrays people stricken with loneliness and sin. Sullivan asserts, rightly, that O'Connor's characters are not evil or innocent. Rather, "The distinctions are between those who know of God's mercy and those who do not, between those who think they can save themselves, either for this life or for the next, and those who are driven, in spite of their own failings, to do God's purpose."[85] "All my stories," she writes, "are about the action of grace on a character who is not very willing to support it."[86] Aside from a need for God, O'Connor's characters long for companionship; however, they repeatedly fail to communicate. For example, out for the day with Sabbath Lily, Haze interrogates her about her father: "How did he come to believe? What changed him into a preacher for Jesus?" Sabbath responds by saying, "I do like a dirt road, particularly when it's hilly like this one here"

---

[81]Ibid., 163.

[82]O'Connor, "The King of the Birds," in *Mystery*, 2.

[83]O'Connor, *Habit of Being*, 350.

[84]Ibid., 69-70.

[85]Sullivan, *Death by Melancholy*, 27.

[86]O'Connor, *Habit of Being*, 275.

(68). O'Connor's humor is undercut by the pathos of such a scene, for tragedy lies in the fact that none of her characters makes linear connections among his or her fellows, and but few reach up to God.

In true New Testament style, vision is a central theme in *Wise Blood.* From the first chapter on, Haze's eyes are mentioned, reminding the reader of everything from *Oedipus* to *King Lear* to the biblical stories of Samson or the Apostle Paul. Mrs. Hitchcock observes Haze's eyes immediately, "like passages leading somewhere" (10). Sabbath later tells her father that she likes Haze's eyes: "They don't look like they see what he's looking at but they keep on looking" (62). Haze, straining to see, ultimately blinds himself as a plea to God to lift his spiritual blindness. Through his loss of sight, Haze, says Sullivan, "turns his vision totally inward away from this world, toward the Christ who exists in the inner darkness."[87] Once more, through violence, a character achieves grace. In what several critics term asceticism and penitence, Haze realizes his hypocrisy and moves into extreme humility. Having lined his shoes with gravel, glass, and stones, Haze walks miles to "pay." Asked what debt he owes, Haze responds, "Mind your business. You can't see" (121). Haze, through suffering, has been given new eyes.

Because of his Calvinistic notion of God and his early exposure to Christ, Haze has set about to deny Jesus. His "waspish" grandfather, we're told, was a circuit preacher, "with Jesus hidden in his head like a stinger" (15). As a young boy he goes to a carnival and is admitted into a tent in which men are watching a nude woman in a casket. His mother confronts him about his activities, and Haze, the reader is told, "forgot the guilt of the tent for the nameless unplaced guilt that was in him" (39). This identification with all sinners forces Haze to do penance after his innocent excursion; Haze then thinks, "That ought to satisfy Him" (39). While in the Army, Haze sets out his attitude toward Christ: "He had all the time he could want to study his soul and assure himself that it was not there. . . . The misery he had was a longing for home; it had nothing to do with Jesus" (18). Years later, when a child hands him a tract that reads "Jesus Calls You," Haze tears it into pieces—unemotionally, methodically.

The transformation from the early Haze to the one who is able to blind himself with quicklime is nothing short of dramatic. An example of Haze's philosophical system follows:

---

[87]Sullivan, *Death by Melancholy,* 27.

(1) It "was not right to believe anything you couldn't see or hold in your hands or test with your teeth" (112).

(2) "There's only one truth and that is that there's no truth" (90).

(3) "In yourself right now is all the place you've got" (90).

(4) "Your conscience is a trick . . . [your conscience is] no more than your face in the mirror is or your shadow behind you" (90-91).

It is Haze's beliefs concerning Christ, however, that O'Connor defines more clearly. "I am clean," says Haze. "If Jesus existed, I wouldn't be clean" (53). Once blinded, Haze humbly acknowledges that he is not clean. What he means in the former assertion, of course, is that if Christ were real, He would demand that Haze be clean (saved). When Haze refuses to believe in sin or in Christ, he saves himself. "Nothing matters but that Jesus don't exist" (33), he says. One might rephrase his comment, "Everything matters if Jesus does exist." Ironically, Jesus is all Haze has, as Enoch Emory notes: "You don't know nobody neither. . . . You ain't got no woman nor nothing to do. I knew when I first seen you you didn't have nobody nor nothing but Jesus. I seen you, and I knew it" (36).

Unlike John Milton with his concept of our right to know or the biblical principle of the Truth that sets us free, for Haze heightened consciousness implies heightened guilt. Even as a child, Haze fled the deity:

> There was already a deep black wordless conviction in him that the way to avoid Jesus was to avoid sin. He knew by the time he was twelve years old that he was going to be a preacher. Later he saw Jesus move from tree to tree in the back of his mind, a wild ragged figure motioning him to turn around and come off into the dark where he might be walking on the water and not know it and then suddenly know it and drown (16).

The knowledge is the damnation, for Haze cannot trust his Maker. To face his soul's need, Haze proceeds in a religious ritual of denial. What he creates is a "new jesus." To provide the new jesus, Haze founds the Church Without Christ, for some a parody of humanistic religions. While crying, "I don't have to run from anything because I don't believe in anything" (45), Haze establishes a new sect: "Well, I preach the Church Without Christ. I'm member and preacher to that church where the blind don't see and the lame don't walk and what's dead stays that way. Ask me about that Church and I'll tell you it's the church that the blood of Jesus don't foul with redemption"

(60). Haze's new religion has no use for sin or redemption, because each necessitates the other: "I'm going to preach there was no Fall because there was nothing to fall from and no Redemption because there was no Fall and no Judgment because there wasn't the first two. Nothing matters but that Jesus was a liar" (60). To a rapt audience, Haze pleads, "What you need is something to take the place of Jesus, something that would speak plain. The Church Without Christ don't have a Jesus but it needs one! It needs a new jesus! It needs one that's all man, without blood to waste. Give me such a jesus, you people" (78).

The only one of Haze's disciples who sets about to obey is Enoch, reputed to have wise blood, or intuition. In a local museum, Enoch discovers a shrunken mummy, which he delivers to Haze. When Haze holds the horrifying, dry object—handed to him by Sabbath in a grotesque parody of the Virgin and Child—he realizes he has found precisely what he sought. The realization stuns him. One critic calls the mummy "Christianity's shrunken vitality,"[88] but this is too simple. The mummy may represent any false god one seeks or, as in Haze's case, an agent of salvation or a representation of one's own shriveled soul. Certainly, Haze comes face to face with the embodiment of his faith, a dried-up mummy.

O'Connor places the finishing critical word on her own creation. In a July 23, 1960, letter, she writes, "That Haze rejects that mummy suggests everything. What he has been looking for with body and soul throughout the book is suddenly presented to him and he sees it has to be rejected, he sees it ain't really what he's looking for."[89] The nihilist travels a wavy route to the scene of his redemption. Holding the sawdust embodiment of his new jesus, Haze must confront the creation of his own mind. His act of penitence then is to blind himself. O'Connor describes his "deep burned eye sockets" which "seemed to lead him into the dark tunnel where he had disappeared" (126). In a New Testament paradox equivalent to the "meek shall inherit the earth," Haze reasons that since he was spiritually blind while he saw the world about him, he should represent his new-found faith by blinding himself physically.

Wise Blood may be read as a tale of the Christian progression through sin, redemption, and awareness into new life. In line with fundamentalist

---

[88]Stuart L. Burns, "The Evolution of *Wise Blood*," *Modern Fiction Studies* 16 (Summer 1970): 154.

[89]O'Connor, *Habit of Being,* 404.

doctrine, Haze is reborn, but a terrifying birth it is. He does, as Mrs. Flood (his landlady) observes, move "backwards to Bethlehem" (119) by means of pain, suffering, and penitence. As Christian allegory, *Wise Blood* teaches the reader the cost of fleeing God, the perils of reclining in pride, and the necessity for a savior. On another allegorical level, the novel parallels McCullers' portrayal of Singer in *The Heart Is a Lonely Hunter*. Singer, for all practical purposes, does not exist. He is simply the creation of those who seek him. His silence is interpreted as wisdom; his presence, as balm. Because others have fashioned Singer in the image of their need, Singer cannot uphold their vision. He is not God—he is a lonely human being. When Haze sets up his new jesus, he has rewritten Christianity to avoid the implications of what O'Connor considers the individual's inherently evil nature. One cannot, we realize, construct a deity and worship him. Nor can one ignore one's own potential for wrongdoing.

Wise Blood is an allegory of one's moving into self-awareness, of the plight of humanity in search of love, of the emptiness of communication, and of the journey that moves into the essence of human nature. Haze's penance is, of course, extreme, but O'Connor does not write realism. The penance he chooses is symbolic of self-annihilation. O'Connor's parable of self-knowledge is not easily ignored, for one's perception is hardly a concern for writers of Scripture or modern theologians alone. Awareness emerges from suffering; people often fail to befriend one another; the gods we place on pedestals often topple. Finally, we cannot forever avoid the ghosts that lurk behind us. Whether we turn and find Christ or not, we must turn. O'Connor's way of seeing the world is rooted in her Christian faith. Her concerns, however, belong to us all.

William Faulkner

Photo courtesy Special Collections, John Davis Williams Library, University of Mississippi, Oxford, Mississippi

Chapter 4

Faulkner's Allegories of the Haunted South

1. The Failed Messiahs of *Go Down, Moses*

The Messiah will come as soon as the most unbridled individualism of faith becomes possible. . . . The Messiah will come only when he is no longer necessary; he will come only on the day after his arrival; he will come, not on the last day, but on the very last.

—Franz Kafka
"The Coming of the Messiah"

And I know you will say now: That if truth is one thing to me and another thing to you, how will we choose which is truth? You don't need to choose. The heart already knows. He didn't have His Book written to be read by what must elect and choose, but by the heart, not by the wise of the earth because maybe the wise no longer have any heart, but by the doomed and lowly of the earth who have nothing else to read with but the heart. Because the men who wrote his Book for Him were writing about truth and there is only one truth and it covers all things that touch the heart.

—William Faulkner
Go Down, Moses

Go Down, Moses is both Faulkner's darkest work and one of his most structurally loose novels. In his review of *Go Down, Moses* in *The New Republic*, Malcolm Cowley called the book a "hybrid: a loosely disjointed but ambitious novel masquerading as a collection of stories, possibly because William Faulkner was too proud or indifferent to call them chapters in a book."[1] Even though Random House is named as the culprit in assigning the original title, *Go Down, Moses and Other Stories* (one which Faulkner later changed), *Go Down, Moses* easily could be taken as a collection of short stories. The chapters shift in point of view, tone, and apparent purpose, and as critic Michael Millgate says, "in period setting, theme, and personnel."[2] Nevertheless, while one may tap into formalist criticism of this text,[3] a strong argument may be made for the success of Faulkner's characterization, juxtaposition, and careful thematic development in the construction of an effective novel of incident. Whatever the case, a discussion of Faulkner as allegorist requires that we look primarily at "The Bear," the much-anthologized short story/chapter. "The Old People," "Delta Autumn," and "Go Down, Moses" are important as well, for they deal directly with Isaac McCaslin and Gavin Stevens, Faulkner's representatives of the Old and New South.

A chronicle that begins with the sport of slave-chasing in "Was" and moves into other sanctioned forms of the hunt, *Go Down, Moses* offers by its very title a plea for deliverance, alluding both to Scripture and to the well-known Negro spiritual. The book ends with the author's assessment of progress in the New South. Here Stevens, with the best of motives and the warmest of hearts, proves to be as ineffectual a leader as Ike McCaslin, who can ultimately do no more than renounce his past. Faulkner himself says of Ike, "Well, I think a man ought to do more than just repudiate. He should have been more affirmative instead of shunning people."[4] In spite of his ultimate defeat, Ike is a magnificent failure. He learns to feel pity for the hunted animal and love for a small, courageous dog. The young hunter learns that courage is not synonymous with ignorance, and he faces the fear in himself, recognizing it as he tastes in his "saliva that taint of brass which he had smelled in the

---

[1] Malcolm Cowley, "Go Down to Faulkner's Land," *The New Republic* 106 (29 June 1942): 900.

[2] Michael Millgate, *The Achievement of William Faulkner* (New York: Random House, 1966) 203.

[3] Among the most comprehensive studies of Faulkner's narrative form in *Go Down, Moses* are James Early's *The Making of Go Down, Moses* (Dallas TX: Southern Methodist University Press, 1972) and Michael Millgate's section on the novel in *Faulkner* (New York: Capricorn Books, 1971).

[4] Quoted in *Lion in the Garden: Interviews with William Faulkner*, eds., James B. Meriwether and Michael Millgate (New York: Random House, 1968) 225.

huddled dogs when he peered under the kitchen."[5] He abandons the implements of civilization—a gun, a watch, and a compass—in order to meet the wilderness on its own terms. Perhaps it is General Compson in "The Bear" who pays Ike his highest tribute:

> And you shut up, Cass. . . . You've got one foot straddled into a farm and the other foot straddled into a bank; you ain't even got a good hand-hold where this boy was already an old man long before you damned Sartorises and Edmondses invented farms and banks to keep yourselves from having to find out what this boy was born knowing and fearing too maybe but without being afraid, that could go ten miles on a compass because he wanted to look at a bear none of us had ever got near enough to put a bullet in and looked at the bear and came the ten miles back on the compass in the dark . . . (250-51).

Although Ike may easily be characterized as idealistic concerning the ownership of land and the nature of humanity, he often demonstrates astonishing perception. When Compson and Walter Ewell decide to form a club and to lease the camp and rent hunting rights, what Faulkner describes is the response of an intensely sensitive Ike: "Even the boy, listening, recognized it for the subterfuge it was: to change the leopard's spots when they could not alter the leopard" (315). The wilderness is shrinking, and Ike knows what his elders will not face—that the dream cannot be prolonged. As an adult, Ike attests to the importance of honesty with oneself ("I have got myself to live with for the rest of my life and all I want is peace to do it in"—288) and to the fallibility of love of land and courage. His understanding of the latter is illustrated in his words to Cass concerning the Civil War:

> Who else [but the South] could have declared a war against a power with ten times the area and a hundred times the men and a thousand times the resources, except men who could believe that all necessary to conduct a successful war was not acumen nor shrewdness nor politics nor diplomacy nor money nor even integrity and simple arithmetic but just love of land and courage (288-89).

---

[5]William Faulkner, *Go Down, Moses* (New York: Random House, 1942) 203. Subsequent references to this work will be cited in the text.

Ike's idealism is buffered with common sense and sensitivity, yet he fails to move a step beyond and put either into action.

Like many of Nathaniel Hawthorne's characters, Ike isolates himself, and in the process he becomes an advocate of death rather than a testimony to the value of life. Hawthorne and Faulkner understood the power and restorative nature of concern for another human being, as Hawthorne demonstrated both fictionally and in his personal life. In a letter to his wife, Sophia, dated October 4, 1840, Hawthorne writes:

> I used to think that I could imagine all passions, all feelings, all states of the heart and mind; but how little did I know what it is to be mingled with another's being! Thou only hast taught me that I have a heart. . . . Thou only hast revealed me to myself; for without thy aid, my best knowledge of myself would have been merely to know my own shadow—to watch it flickering on the wall, and mistake its fantasies for my own real actions. Indeed, we are but shadows—we are not endowed with real life, and all that seems most real about us is but the thinnest substance of a dream—till the heart is touched. That touch creates us.[6]

In the end, Ike's fear supersedes his love as he longs to understand himself and his past; *Go Down, Moses* thereby becomes a fictional cry for a savior. Both Ike and Stevens fail to rescue those around them: Ike lies in an attitude of death at the end of "Delta Autumn," hands crossed over his breast, listening to the "grieving rain" (365); Stevens brings home the body of one more victim of injustice, prejudice, and fear. Faulkner draws insistent parallels between his protagonists and the Bible in the title *Go Down, Moses* alone, and he intensifies comparisons between Ike and Christ and refers often to Stevens as a possible Deliverer for the New South. While Faulkner graphically describes Ike's failures in "The Bear" and "Delta Autumn," it is Ike's obsession with the wilderness that best reveals his fragmented self. In *A Study of History*, Arnold Toynbee deals with the wilderness as a place for escape, healing; however, he distinguishes between simple detachment and the transfiguration of self and society possible through what he terms "withdrawal-and-return." It is through

---

[6]Cited in *The Portable Hawthorne*, ed. Malcolm Cowley (New York: Viking Press, 1969) 674.

Toynbee's examination of the wilderness that one may best understand the extent of Ike's crime against himself and his fellows.

Toynbee writes that a "transfiguration in solitude can have no purpose, and perhaps even no meaning, except as a prelude to the return of the transfigured person." He adds that "the human social animal cannot permanently estrange himself without repudiating his humanity and becoming, in Aristotle's phrase, 'either a beast or a god.' "[7] The "logical goal" of total detachment, Toynbee asserts, is self-annihilation.[8] In "Delta Autumn," Ike fails to defend himself from two onslaughts. Faced by Edmonds at the campfire, Ike announces his belief that most men are a "little better than their circumstances give them a chance to be." Edmonds replies, "So you've lived almost eighty years and that's what you finally learned about the other animals you lived among. I suppose the question to ask you is, where have you been all the time you were dead?" (345).

Earlier in the novel, the reader is told that Ike is "insulated by his years and time from the corruption of steel and oiled moving parts which tainted the others" (342). But one must not assume that Faulkner is purifying Ike, for he also insulates himself from empathy, from involvement with others. His ultimate test—the confrontation with the mulatto woman—reveals Ike's deepest nature. When Ike offers her Roth Edmonds' bribe in "Delta Autumn," he cries, "Take it out of my tent"; her leaving will not save him any more than repudiating his inheritance kept him from being tainted by the past. Ike condemns himself further with the plea, "Marry a black man. . . . Then you will forget all this, forget it ever happened" (363). The woman responds, as Edmonds had earlier, mocking the negligible wisdom Ike gained over the years: "Old man . . . have you lived so long and forgotten so much that you don't remember anything you ever knew or felt or even heard about love?" (363). Toynbee clarifies Ike's struggles with his fellows through the observation that "perfect detachment casts out pity, and therefore also love, as inexorably as it purges away all the evil passions."[9]

Ike surrenders to the wilderness, but he never emerges. Faulkner describes Ike in "The Bear" as standing for a "moment—a child alien and lost in the green and soaring gloom of the markless wilderness. Then he

---

[7]Arnold J. Toynbee, *A Study of History, Vol. I-VI,* ed. D. C. Somervell (New York: Oxford University Press, 1947) 217.

[8]Ibid., 527.

[9]Ibid.

relinquished completely to it" (208). But it is Ike's desire to remain in the wilderness that ultimately damns him. He tries to repudiate the land left him by his father and Uncle Buddy (256); he cries out to Cass for rest and peace from the world; and he speaks of the endurance of the black race as opposed to the frailty of his own, "a longer time free than us because we have never been free" (295). Aware of his condition, he can do nothing but isolate himself and wander in the wilderness, his "mistress and his wife" (326), a wilderness that "soared, musing, inattentive, myriad, eternal, green" (322).

Yet within the link Faulkner makes between Ike and Christ lies the most profound condemnation of Ike's wilderness existence and his disassociation with his world:

> If the Nazarene had found carpentering good for the life and ends
> He had assumed and elected to serve, it would be all right too for
> Isaac McCaslin even though Isaac McCaslin's ends, although
> simple enough in their apparent motivation, were and would be
> always incomprehensible to him, and his life, invincible enough in
> its needs, if he could have helped himself, not being the Nazarene,
> he would not have chosen it: and paid it back (309-10).

Ike is oblivious to his mission, his reason for relating with those around him. His motivations and prejudices remain incomprehensible to him even until the final scene of "Delta Autumn." Toynbee emphasizes Christ's withdrawal in the wilderness and at Gethsemane, but he makes it clear that Christ had become "conscious of his mission" at his baptism and had returned from his forty days of wandering and temptation "in the power of the spirit."[10] Rather than conquering with the sword or avoiding his culture, Christ determined to die on the cross: "In choosing this alternative in the hour of crisis, Jesus is breaking . . . away from the conventional line of action taken by other would-be saviors."[11] On the other hand, Ike, father to no one, has nothing human that he loves enough to live or to die for. Toynbee notes,

> If the Founder of the Christian religion and his apostle-missionary
> Paul had been addicts to the philosophy of detachment, they would
> have remained in their wilderness for the rest of their lives on

---

[10]Ibid., 222.
[11]Ibid., 544.

Earth. The limitation of the philosophy of detachment is its failure to see that its Nirvana is not the terminus of the Soul's journey but merely a station on its route. The terminus is the Kingdom of God; and this omnipresent Kingdom calls for service from its citizens on Earth here and now.[12]

The wilderness is traditionally the place in which God meets his creation: Israelites find bread and water, Moses encounters a burning bush, Hagar and Ishmael—ostracized at Sarah's request—claim God's promise of protection, and David and Saul are reconciled. After Jesus' temptation in the desert, he began to proclaim the message: "Repent: for the kingdom of heaven is at hand" (Matt 4:17b). Having faced the dark forces of human nature in the wilderness, Christ returns to society stronger, more determined, and more fully savior. While Ike is initiated in the wilderness, he learns only a few of its lessons. His failures intensify the pathos of Gavin Steven's comment concerning Samuel Worsham Beauchamp, "sold into Egypt": "And that's who I am to find, save" (371). However, in *Go Down, Moses*, Stevens cannot save the twenty-six-year-old victim of the South, Ike cannot save himself, and neither, finally, can redeem his present or explain his past.

Between 1926 and 1942 Faulkner published eleven works with Southern themes. Certainly, the themes of prejudice, cruelty, miscegenation, and loss of ancestry and heritage may be found once again in *Go Down, Moses*, but in this novel, as in *Light in August*, the South becomes a microcosm for the world. Faulkner once called *Moby-Dick* an "allegory of moral consciousness";[13] *Go Down, Moses* is no less. Too many critics term Faulkner a realist or a naturalist and consider *A Fable* his only true allegory. While *Light in August* employs more allegorical devices than *Go Down, Moses*, the title of the novel alone is as rich in implications as "The Bear" is in symbols. To fail to see this is to omit Faulkner from a long line of allegorists. Lewis Leary provides such a partial list:

> Like the Melville whom Lawrance Thompson once disclosed as having so intense a "quarrel with God" that he dared not express it directly, like the Hawthorne whose *The Scarlet Letter* has been interpreted in a dozen ways, like the Henry James whom Quentin

---

[12]Ibid., 531.
[13]Quoted in *Lion in the Garden*, 247.

Anderson has discovered to be a devious deviser of parables, or like Katherine Anne Porter who delights with indirection, Faulkner also suggests more than he ever says.[14]

Walter Sullivan comes the closest of any critic to defining Faulkner's didactic tendencies, to revealing his message. With characteristic bluntness, Sullivan writes:

What Faulkner, in his major phase, told us about life was simply the truth. He showed us that man was flawed and that out of mankind's fallen condition issued certain hurts and disappointments, perfidies, and deceptions, which at best could only be partially healed, imperfectly redeemed within the earthly circumstance. Finally, when the difficulties of life became too much for us, when we found that our mere human strength and endurance were no longer sufficient to support the tragic reality, we denied reality: we turned our backs on the truth.[15]

While more than skeptical of our ability to save ourselves or remake history, Faulkner nonetheless reaches out for the eternal qualities of honor, courage, compassion, and justice. Failing to find a savior, he nevertheless seeks what F. W. Dillistone terms "individual manifestations of such compassion and sacrifice as are capable of redeeming." "In them and through them," Dillistone writes, people "regain their birthright within the human race."[16] Though this quest is thwarted at every turn in *Go Down, Moses*, Dilsey of *The Sound and the Fury* and Gail Hightower, Byron Bunch, and Lena Grove of *Light in August* testify to more than a flickering candle in the dark center of Faulkner's fiction.

Without an understanding of Faulkner's intent, one might stumble into various misconceptions of Ike McCaslin. Some interpretations cannot be supported at all by the text; others fail to consider Ike in terms of the corpus of Faulkner's work. One of the former errors is committed by R. D.

---

[14]Lewis Leary, *Southern Excursions* (Baton Rouge LA: Louisiana State University Press, 1971) 212-13.

[15]Walter Sullivan, *Death by Melancholy: Essays on Modern Southern Fiction* (Baton Rouge: Louisiana State University Press, 1972) 19-20.

[16]F. W. Dillistone, *The Novelist and the Passion Story* (New York: Sheed and Ward, 1960) 108.

Ackermann, who writes, "There is no question that Faulkner's sympathies here are with the girl [the mulatto woman of "Delta Autumn"], with nature, and finally with Ike, who, as a priest of the God of nature, sanctifies this sexual union and blesses its offspring."[17] Ike is tormented in "Delta Autumn" by the realization that Roth has fathered a child by a mulatto, stunned that he himself is her uncle, and can only tell her to take Roth's money and marry a black man. Nowhere is Ike a priest; nowhere is there blessing for Roth's newborn son. By noting Christian imagery and parallels between Ike and Christ, Carol Harter asserts, "In the final analysis, Isaac McCaslin represents the end of a long line of deluding and self-deluded men enmeshed in a culture and heritage marred by corruption and failure."[18]

Unfortunately, her view is overbalanced by critics such as Ursula Brumm, who oversimplifies Ike's life by seeing his renunciation of property as an imitation of Christ. Faulkner himself explains that Ike does not understand even the good he does and testifies to the significance of this ignorance. Ike's abdication from history and his insistence on few possessions (including only carpenter's tools, a compass, and an iron cot and mattress) do not indicate moral purity. They do indicate fear, shame. Christ operated among his fellows with a singular sense of purpose, recruiting disciples, overturning the tables of the moneychangers in the Temple, and arguing with religious leaders concerning Scripture. One can admire Ike only partially for what he abstains from. Because of Ike's honesty and awareness of injury to others, it remains far too easy to fall prey to the assessment of Robert Detweiler and others. Detweiler calls Ike an "example of the prototype of the good man who is true to the nature outside and within him and who can thereby remain whole in a broken world."[19] Yet is it Ike's very incompleteness that Faulkner reveals: He cannot be a Moses for the Israelites around him, for he has compromised his own personal search. Finally, a few critics such as Albert Devlin fail by reduction. Devlin, for example, sees Ike's inability to act as a result of a cold,

---

[17]R. D. Ackermann, "The Immolation of Isaac McCaslin," *Texas Studies in Language and Literature* 16 (Fall 1974): 564.

[18]Carol Harter, "The Winter of Isaac McCaslin: Revisions and Irony in Faulkner's 'Delta Autumn,' " *Journal of Modern Literature* 1 (1970): 225.

[19]Robert Detweiler, "Christ and the Christ Figure in American Fiction," *The Christian Scholar* 47 (1964): 115.

domineering mother and wife.[20] Faulkner, however, does not set Ike up as a complicated puzzle. Clues meet our eyes at every turn.

The first hint of Ike's nature appears in the first sentence of the first chapter, entitled "Was." The title is, of course, ironic, for the Old South pictured in this chapter is far from past tense. Ike is introduced only as one who has heard the story from his cousin, Cass Edmonds, sixteen years older than he. In "Was," twin brothers, Buddy and Buck, pursue a runaway slave, Thomasina's Terrel, to a neighboring plantation, ironically named "Warwick." The pursuit is a game, inevitable because Terrel is in love with Tennie, a slave woman. By the end of the horrifying tale told in a comic tone, Buck (who later will father Ike) has been caught by the mistress of Warwick, Sophonsiba, and Terrel and Tennie are united after being the pawns in a card game. Faulkner's tone is revealed even in seemingly lighthearted events through incidents such as a $500 bet on where Terrel will be found after dark, a card game that determines the fate of two who love one another, and lines that describe the slave hunt as sport: "It wasn't any race at all" (15).

In the first line of "Was," Ike is described as a "widower now and uncle to half a county and father to no one" (3). Ike, as isolated as any of Faulkner's characters, is wed only to the wilderness, for the settled earth is sign and symbol of his family's guilt. On the first page the reader learns that Ike "owned no property and never desired to since the earth was no man's but all men's" (3). Considering himself coeval with the wilderness, an aging Ike sees the dissolution of the only thing he loves—"the land across which there came now no scream of panther but instead the long hooting of locomotives" (341). In fact, it is Ike's attachment to the land that gives him honor:

> Because it was his land, although he had never owned a foot of it. He had never wanted to, not even after he saw plain its ultimate doom, watching it retreat year by year before the onslaught of axe and saw and log-lines and then dynamite and tractor plows, because it belonged to no man. It belonged to all; they had only to use it well, humbly and with pride (353-54).

But love of land, one learns later in the novel, is not enough. After "The Fire and the Hearth" and "Pantaloon in Black," the reader meets Ike as

---

[20]Albert Devlin, " 'How Much It Takes to Compound a Man': A Neglected Scene in *Go Down, Moses,*" *The Midwest Quarterly* 14 (Summer 1973): 408-21.

a youth. In "The Old People," Ike, twelve years old, kills his first buck and is baptized by his spiritual parent, Sam Fathers, a man of both Indian and Negro descent. Ike pulled the head of the buck back and the "throat taut and drew Sam Fathers' knife across the throat and Sam stooped and dipped his hands in the hot smoking blood and wiped them back and forth across the boy's face" (164). Here, Ike gains an "unforgettable sense of the big woods" (175) and, as Faulkner tells us, ceases to be a "child and [becomes] a hunter and a man" (178). The McCaslin pride in the inheritance of land is revealed in "The Old People." Faulkner tells us that the hold of Ike's family on the land "actually was as trivial and without reality as the now faded and archaic script in the chancery book in Jefferson which allocated it to them" (171). The wilderness also is juxtaposed here to the settled land as Faulkner begins the chapter with the words, "At first there was nothing" (163). He reminds us midway through the chapter: "And again there was nothing" (181). The wilderness takes on a mythical quality, a supremacy, an omniscience: "Then, as if it had waited for them to find their positions and become still, the wilderness breathed again" (181).

"The Bear" remains the strongest chapter and functions as both an account of Ike's second trip into the wilderness and as a historical chronicle of the crimes of Ike's family. The allegorical qualities of the chapter are undeniable. The first sentence of "The Bear" reminds one of parable, for Faulkner chooses a storytelling style similar to D. H. Lawrence's in "Rocking-Horse Winner" and *A Man Who Died*: "There was a man and a dog too this time" (191). In this chapter, of course, Ike also meets Old Ben, a "taintless and incorruptible" (191) symbol of the wilderness and all that is inviolable and courageous in humanity itself. In typical Faulknerian prose, the reader meets the bear: ". . . a corridor of wreckage and destruction beginning back before the boy was born, through which sped, not fast but rather with the ruthless and irresistible deliberation of a locomotive, the shaggy tremendous shape" (193).

The bear clearly moves Faulkner out of the range of critics who would like to nail him as a realist or even naturalist. Old Ben, Faulkner writes, "ran in [Ike's] knowledge before he ever saw it":

> It loomed and towered in his dreams before he even saw the unaxed
> woods where it left its crooked print, shaggy, tremendous, red-eyed,
> not malevolent but just big, too big for the dogs which tried to bay
> it, for the horses which tried to ride it down, for the men and the

bullets they fired into it; too big for the very country which was its
constricting scope (193).

Lest one miss the implications of such a beast or the reverberations of such a
symbol, Faulkner writes of a wilderness "through which ran not even a mortal
beast but an anachronism, indomitable and invincible out of an old dead time,
a phantom, epitome and apotheosis of the old wild life which the little puny
humans swarmed and hacked at in a fury of abhorrence and fear like pygmies
about the ankles of a drowsing elephant" (193). Sam makes the bear all-
knowing when he warns Ike that Old Ben knows he has joined the hunting
squad: "If Old Ben gets hemmed up and has got to pick out somebody to run
over, he will pick out you" (201). When Ike finally corners the bear, Faulkner
refers to the beast as "it" eight times in nine lines. This and other aspects of his
prose reveal the existence of a small boy in the face of a towering Presence: "It
did not emerge, appear: it was just there, immobile, fixed in the green and
windless noon's hot dappling, not as big as he had dreamed it but as big as he
had expected, bigger, dimensionless against the dappled obscurity, looking at
him. Then it moved . . . " (209). The bear is felled, not by a modern weapon
but by Boon Hogganbeck and his dog Lion. Lion dies soon after, as does an
aged Sam Fathers—Lion of his wounds, Sam perhaps by request at Boon's
hands.

    Ike becomes an actor in an allegory the moment Faulkner creates the
wilderness and its terrifying Inhabitant as larger than life. Symbols in this
section are as common and complex as in *Wise Blood* or *Light in August*. When
Ike moves into the wilderness before dawn seeking Old Ben, he carries a
compass (a gift from Cass), a watch (his father's), and a stick for snakes. The
accoutrements of civilization are obvious, and the reader is then told,

> He had already relinquished, of his will, because of his need, in
> humility and peace and without regret, yet apparently that had not
> been enough, the leaving of the gun was not enough. He stood for
> a moment—a child, alien and lost in the green and soaring gloom
> of the markless wilderness. Then he relinquished completely to it.
> It was the watch and the compass. He was still tainted. He removed
> the linked chain of the one and the looped thong of the other from
> his overalls and hung them on a bush and leaned the stick beside
> them and entered it (208).

Ike must surrender to the wilderness, to his fear, to a newly found belief in self—the possibilities are endless. The bear appears when Ike is most vulnerable and hopeful. Whatever key the reader chooses for the symbolic system, the tale functions as a traditional initiation. "It seemed to him," writes Faulkner of Ike, "that at the age of ten he was witnessing his own birth. It was not even strange to him. He had experienced it all before, and not merely in dreams" (195).

Again in "The Bear" Ike consecrates the wilderness and repudiates the land his family has acquired. The land takes on allegorical significance as well, for it represents not only human pride in the material but the cumulative guilt of all humanity. When Ike turns his back on the land of his fathers, he is setting up a kind of Church Without Christ. If he can repudiate his inheritance as Haze repudiates Jesus—if he denies his part in the family, the culture—then he purifies himself morally. Yet Faulkner reminds the reader of Ike's need to act in the face of his guilt to counteract the effects of his family's existence upon the earth. The wilderness is described as the world through which "frail and timorous man had merely passed without altering it, leaving no mark nor scar" (202). Such is not the case with history or the land that became farms or plantations. An older Ike tells Cass how the earth was intended by God:

> He made the earth first and peopled it with dumb creatures, and then He created man to be His overseer on the earth and to hold suzerainty over the earth and the animals on it in His name, not to hold for himself and his descendants inviolable title forever, generation after generation, to the oblongs and squares of the earth (257).

Much of Ike's anger turns toward his grandfather, Carothers McCaslin, from whose hands comes the "tamed land which was to have been [Ike's] heritage" (254). Carothers McCaslin's pride in his ownership of land repels Ike, for not only could the Indian Ikkemotubbe not sell the land he never owned, but McCaslin produced his crops with the labor of slaves. Ike tells Cass despairingly:

> I can't repudiate it. It was never mine to repudiate. It was never Father's and Uncle Buddy's to bequeath me. . . . Because it was never Ikkemotubbe's fathers' fathers' to bequeath Ikkemotubbe to sell to Grandfather or any man because on the instant when

Ikkemotubbe discovered, realised, that he could sell it for money, on that instant it ceased ever to have been his forever, father to father to father, and the man who bought it bought nothing (256-57).

The exchange of money for crops raised by slaves angers Ike as well:

> . . . the human beings [Carothers McCaslin] held in bondage and in the power of life and death had removed the forest from it and in their sweat scratched the surface of it to a depth of perhaps fourteen inches in order to grow something out of it which had not been there before and which could be translated back into the money he who believed he had bought it had had to pay to get it and hold it and a reasonable profit too (254).

By refusing his inheritance, Ike tries to leave behind the crimes of his ancestors. Drawn mysteriously to ledgers kept by Carothers and his sons, Buck and Buddy, Ike unravels the first sin in a long line of atrocities committed by his family. The ledgers, which reveal primarily the purchase and sale of slaves, reflect also the death of Eunice, wife of a slave Thucydides. The woman had drowned herself in a creek on Christmas Day 1832. What Ike discovers is that Eunice had given birth to Carothers McCaslin's child, Tomasina (called Tomey), although the ledger records her father as Thucydides. Born in 1810, Tomasina dies during childbirth at the age of twenty-three. Ike, horror-stricken, realizes that the father of Tomasina's son, Terrel, is also Carothers McCaslin—Tomasina's own father. Six months after Eunice discovered Tomey was pregnant with her father's baby, Tomasina dies. Terrel, listed as "son of Thucydus and Eunice," is born in June of 1833. Of Ike, Faulkner writes,

> Looking down at the yellowed page spread beneath the yellow glow of the lantern smoking and stinking in that rank chill midnight room fifty years later, he seemed to see her actually walking into the icy creek on that Christmas day six months before her daughter's and her lover's (Her first lover's he thought. Her first) child was born, solitary, inflexible, griefless, ceremonial, in formal and succinct repudiation of grief and despair who had already had to repudiate belief and hope (271).

Ike's identification with the slave woman testifies to his humanity and perception, and his anger strikes one as nothing if not righteous. Carothers McCaslin sets up a trust of $1,000 for Tomey's Terrel. Carothers, Faulkner writes, "made no effort either to explain or obfuscate the thousand-dollar legacy to the son of an unmarried slave-girl, to be paid only at the child's coming of age, bearing the consequence of the act of which there was still no definite incontrovertible proof that he acknowledged" (269). "So I reckon that was cheaper than saying My son to a nigger," Ike thinks. "Even if My son wasn't but just two words" (269-70). A guilt-ridden Ike cries to Cass, "Don't you see? This whole land, the whole South, is cursed, and all of us who derive from it, whom it ever suckled, white and black both, lie under the curse?" (278). Not such a far cry from the Original Sin of the Calvinist, this view of humanity increases Ike's despair, yet he does not pray. Instead, he renounces his land, living while married in a bungalow his wife's father provided and later in a rented room in Jefferson, Mississippi. He is living in the latter when Lucas Quintus Carothers McCaslin Beauchamp, son of Tomey's Terrel and Tennie Beauchamp, appears in the doorway and asks—on his twenty-first birthday— for the remainder of Carothers McCaslin's money. Ike realizes then that only a part of what he flees is the land he has renounced. The rest, with a human face and human voice, visits him in the form of Lucas Beauchamp and later in the form of Roth's woman in "Delta Autumn."

It is an old and defeated Ike McCaslin who greets the reader in "Delta Autumn." As T. H. Adamowski writes in an article appropriately titled "Isaac McCaslin and the Wilderness of the Imagination," Ike is "always alone, and his rite of autumn is a private one."[21] In our final view of Ike, he is moving undeniably toward death: "McCaslin lay back down, the blanket once more drawn to his chin, his crossed hands once more weightless on his breast in the empty tent" (365). Ike's guilt lies in his self-delusion, a characteristic Harter finds central to his "consciously trying to emulate Christ for the ultimate sake of an abstract commitment to this concept of 'communal brotherhood' and, in so doing, renders himself effectual only in terms of the 'Word,' while he becomes increasingly impotent in his ability to accomplish the 'Deed.' "[22] She adds, "Because McCaslin believes that he has 'righted a wrong' in the [very] act

---

[21]T. H. Adamowski, "Isaac McCaslin and the Wilderness of the Imagination," *The Centennial Review* 17 (Winter 1973): 112.

[22]Harter, "The Winter of Isaac McCaslin," 214.

of repudiation, he has consequently deluded himself into believing that his abnegation has indeed enabled" him to transcend.[23] One's empathy with Ike may be largely an identification with his loss of innocence from the time of the hunt. A 1982 book on modern Southern literature by Daniel Joseph Singal claims that Faulkner's "demonic vision was most frequently the image of southern innocence violated."[24] In the chapter "William Faulkner and the Discovery of Southern Evil," Singal argues that the past for the Southerner was no longer glorious but soiled with sin and pain:

> What stood revealed was a South tormented and paralyzed, trapped in an intricate web largely of its own making, which tied together sexuality, avarice, and aggression with the "higher" facets of southern life until they were all hopelessly tangled. Instead of a repository of glory and innocence, the past was now seen as a fatalistic curse upon the present that no southerner could wholly escape.[25]

Ike, with his honesty and sensitivity, was the only hope for his world. The New South looks to men such as Gavin Stevens, Faulkner implies, and is no better off. Stevens is called upon to locate Samuel Worsham Beauchamp; his grandmother, Mollie, is a servant on Roth Edmonds' farm. Mollie turns to Stevens, an attorney, to prosecute Edmonds who, she says, "sold my Benjamin. Sold him into Egypt" (371). The epitome of success, Stevens is a Phi Beta Kappa Ph. D. (Heidelberg); however, Faulkner tips the reader off concerning Stevens' effectiveness in his world by relaying one minute fact. Stevens' major project is a "twenty-two-year-old unfinished translation of the Old Testament back into classic Greek" (371). To this man comes the task of rescuing Samuel, who at nineteen was gambling, fighting, and robbing local stores and who by his early twenties had been indicted for the murder of a Chicago policeman. Stevens does not shirk the task of bringing Samuel home. Lying to Mollie and Miss Worsham about the cost of the funeral for Samuel, who is to be executed, Stevens collects money from the townspeople and provides the rest himself. He

---

[23]Ibid., 216.

[24]Daniel Joseph Singal, *The War Within (From Victorian to Modernist Thought in the South, 1919–1945)* (Chapel Hill NC: University of North Carolina Press, 1982) 155.

[25]Ibid., 154.

also makes the editor of the local paper agree not to publish the story of Beauchamp in his hometown. When Stevens tells Mollie and Miss Worsham of Samuel's death, they begin to wail and chant; Stevens flees. "He went down the hall fast, almost running," Faulkner writes. " 'Soon I will be outside,' he thought. 'Then there will be air, space, breath' " (380). Stevens cannot face the reality of their suffering, and it is as unlikely that he will alter the course of history as that Ike could have.

Singal portrays Faulkner's New South by describing Jason Compson of *The Sound and the Fury.* Having tyrannized Caddy and her daughter Quentin, the business-oriented Jason demonstrates what Singal terms "swaggering pride and essential helplessness."[26] When Jason finally is outsmarted by his niece, Faulkner leaves him stunned and empty. The New South, Singal reminds us, is Jason, "lying helpless on the floor, his hands in his pockets."[27] He adds:

> When Jason, Quentin, and Caddy have been pared away, each meeting an inglorious end, what have we left for the white South's future? Faulkner's answer in *The Sound and the Fury* is Benjy, the ultimate example of identity diffusion, the final extension of the isolation and lack of continuity afflicting the other Compson children.[28]

Benjy cannot speak; he cannot articulate his own need, much less reach out to heal another. The characters of Faulkner's fictional world long for a Moses who will lead the people from enslavement. Abraham Lincoln pronounced the blacks free, but *Go Down, Moses* is concerned with the salvation of all the oppressed of the world. Who will save the white race from themselves? From their past? Who will move beyond the flawed natures of Ike and Stevens to alter the culture? The consistently dark vision of *Go Down, Moses* is made more terrible by the longing for hope. "Courage and honor and pride and pity and love of justice and of liberty," Cass says to Ike in "The Bear." "They all touch the heart, and what the heart holds to becomes truth, as far as we know truth" (297). Ike cries for the mother of Roth's child to marry a black man and to take Roth's money out of his tent; Stevens flees a house of sorrow telling Miss

---

[26]Ibid., 179.
[27]Ibid.
[28]Ibid., 179-80.

Worsham he should not have come. Where, the novel implies, is our Moses, our Christ?

2. "Shadows of the Ruined Garden": Transformation in *Light in August*

The fiend in his own shape is less hideous than when he rages in the breast of man.
—Nathaniel Hawthorne
"Young Goodman Brown"

As a Southern writer, [Faulkner] makes the ironic point that man will transcend his plight in the world only when he ceases to resist the Negro in him, that is, when he admits his capacity for love, humility, and sacrifice. The Negro in Christmas and in any man is his capacity to endure the hurt for which man is destined.[29]
—Edwin Moseley
Pseudonyms of Christ in the Modern Novel

While *Go Down, Moses* has been argued to be Faulkner's darkest novel, it is through *Light in August* that one may glimpse the promise of deliverance. It is, ironically, a statement by Cass Edmonds in "The Old People" (*Go Down, Moses*) that best explains the hope one finds in Faulkner's earlier novel:

> And even suffering and grieving is better than nothing; there is only one thing worse than not being alive, and that's shame. But you can't be alive forever, and you always wear out life long before you have exhausted the possibilities of living. And all that must be somewhere; all that could not have been invented and created just to be thrown away (186).

Gail Hightower of *Light in August* suffers and grieves; he also ultimately leaves behind his volume of lofty Alfred Lord Tennyson poetry in favor of the active dramas of William Shakespeare. Embittered and isolated by shame concerning his ancestors and his wife, Hightower gains hope through his involvement with

---

[29]Edwin Moseley, *Pseudonyms of Christ in the Modern Novel* (Pittsburgh: University of Pittsburgh, 1962) 148.

the child of Lena Grove and with Joe Christmas. But the promised light is shadowed by the figure of Joe Christmas, who suffers and grieves and flails against an incomprehensible environment that has failed to define him. Certainly, the end Christmas meets emphasizes, through contrast, the new life Hightower finds.

When William Faulkner explained his structural technique, he focused on character: "I would say [the text] develops itself. It begins with a character, usually, and once he stands up on his feet and begins to move all I do is to trot along behind him with a paper and pencil trying to keep up long enough to put down what he says and does. . . . The characters themselves, they do what they do, not me."[30] *Light in August* is a novel of character: Gail Hightower, an isolated minister seated at his darkened window, and Joe Christmas, an ironic Christ figure struggling to save himself, strive for moments of self-awareness as Faulkner charts their courses through the cycles of dawns and twilights.

Names, of course, play an important role in characterization in any work, but they are central to *Light in August*. Faulkner, here a true servant of allegory, is deliberate in his choice of names. Until he confronts himself, Gail Hightower does not become a "man"—hence his feminine first name (certainly, feminist critics deplore Faulkner's implication here). Also, he is wrenched apart by the turbulence of his past—hence the allusion to a "gale." The significance of his last name becomes clearer as the former minister avoids contact with all but one of his townspeople.

The name Joe Christmas is, of course, ironic. Abandoned in December as an infant, the child is arbitrarily dubbed Joe, which suggests Joseph, father of Jesus, and Christmas, for the season. One cannot avoid the memory of the birth in a Bethlehem manger of a baby the disciples would call the Son of God. Yet even this child—feared and hunted by Herod from birth and executed as a young man—is respected by groups of people across the globe. Christmas has no followers. Other names, such as Joanna Burden (who believes she is pregnant and who is weighted by the shame of racism in the South) and Percy Grimm (who kills Christmas), also are highly connotative. Certainly, Faulkner sets up an allegorical structure with an inherent emphasis on naming.

---

[30]Quoted in *Faulkner at West Point*, eds., Joseph L. Fant and Robert Ashley (New York: Random House, 1964) 111.

Light in August is a seminal work, for here one sees, even more clearly than in the obvious attempt at parable in *A Fable*, an allegorical superstructure in which hope survives. While Christianity as a code of behavior is ignored and the Church withers as an agent of salvation, the figure of the sacrificial Christ dominates the text—so much so that Faulkner changed the title from *Dark House* to *Light in August*. It is a dim light, the copper light of a late August afternoon in Mississippi, but a light it is.

Many critics have turned to Lena Grove (whose first name means "light") as the bearer and representation of whatever salvation may be sought in the novel. In his chapter "Christ as Social Scapegoat," Moseley makes clear the parallels between Lena and Mary, mother of Christ, who seeks a place in Herod's kingdom for the child to be born.[31] Lena is also the diminutive of Magdalene and Helen, the Christian and Greek names for love and femaleness. This study, however, will concentrate instead on Hightower's movement into life and on the ambiguous results of coming into consciousness. It also will deal with several elements of allegory: (1) Hightower and Christmas and their quests (complicated by the ineffectiveness of the Church), (2) the suggestive names Faulkner employs throughout the novel, (3) the network of symbols, and (4) the Christ imagery prevalent in the text.

Faulkner moves beyond what readers might expect to find when they analyze the names imposed on characters in an allegory. Words, for Faulkner, are deterministic. Christmas is named, for example, yet he internalizes the terms even without verifying their truth. Beyond the allegorical significance of his given name, Christmas is called "nigger" by children and by the dietitian at the orphanage. He then allows the word to shape his fate, to create truth. When Joanna Burden asks him how he knows he is a mulatto, Christmas replies, "I don't know it. . . . If I'm not, damned if I haven't wasted a lot of time."[32] Christmas believes he is part black and becomes a divided self; he believes he has killed McEachern and flees. Truth becomes irrelevant in Faulkner's novel, for what humanity perceives to be true is true. Faulkner writes of gossip in the Southern town: "Because that was all [that was] required: that idea, that single idle word blown from mind to mind" (66). In the beginning was the Word and the Word was. Whereas for Byron Bunch

---

[31]Moseley, *Pseudonyms of Christ*, 140.

[32]William Faulkner, *Light in August* (New York: Random House, 1932) 467. Subsequent references to this work will be cited in the text.

words eventually become arbitrary signs ("You are just the one that calls yourself Byron Bunch today, now, this minute"—402), he predicts the effect of Christmas' name early in the novel: "And that was the first time Byron remembered that he had ever thought how a man's name, which is supposed to be just the sound for who he is, can be somehow an augur of what he will do, if other men can only read the meaning in time" (29).

Naming is important allegorically, but it also contributes to the ironic connection between Christmas and Christ himself. Christ often utilized the human necessity to name in order to understand, and names and name changes are repeatedly significant in Scripture. The following dialogue between Simon Peter and Christ appears in Matthew 16:13-16:

> When Jesus came into the coasts of Caesarea Philippi, he asked his disciples, saying, Whom do men say that I the son of man am?
> And they said, Some say that thou art John the Baptist: some, Elias; and others, Jeremias, or one of the prophets.
> He saith unto them, But whom say ye that I am?
> And Simon Peter answered and said, Thou art the Christ, the Son of the living God.

The process of naming involves the process of giving identity, of indicating personal destiny, and of demonstrating understanding of the role and purpose of another.

In addition to an examination of the names Faulkner has chosen, one also must consider the numerous references in *Light in August* to the Christian mythos. The symbolic structure of the novel, as well as the Christ imagery, relies on Scripture for meaning. Fraught with censorship of the Church's role in the modern world (Hightower, for example, is described as having been "denied by his Church" —44), *Light in August* also reflects the thought of a writer grounded in his Christ-haunted culture. The number 7, representing perfection in the Bible, is parodied in the novel. We are told, for example, that the mill in Lena's early life "had been there seven years and in seven years more it would destroy all the timber within its reach" (2). Later, Christmas flees from the law for seven empty days: "And yet I have been further in these seven days than in all the thirty years. . . . But I have never got outside that circle. I have never broken out of the ring of what I have already done and cannot ever undo" (321). The sacrificial lamb, so much a part of the Old Testament prophecy and the references to Jesus in the New Testament, plays a dominant role as well. Lena, the reader learns, is "sheeplike" (4). Later, Christmas associates the menstruation of a woman with his own humanity and predilection to sin. He remembers a "slain sheep, the price paid for immunity" (177), and sex and women and blood and sin and religion twist inextricably in his mind.

If it is not enough that Lena's face has an "inwardlighted quality" (15), she also carries a palm leaf fan when pregnant ("The woman had now gone on, slowly, with her swelling and unmistakable burden"—7). The palm leaf is reminiscent of Jesus' ride into Jerusalem. She also meets Armstid, who takes the travel-worn, pregnant Lena home to his wife Martha. "I reckon I do know what Martha's going to say," Armstid thinks. "I reckon womenfolks are likely to be good without being very kind" (10). When Lena speaks softly of looking for the man she slept with until she finds him, she says to Martha, "I reckon a family ought to all be together when a chap comes. Specially the first one. I reckon the Lord will see to that." Martha responds, "savagely, harshly": "And I reckon He will have to" (18). Beyond Martha's lack of hospitality toward the pregnant Lena (which will remind the reader of the lack of courtesy shown to Mary and Joseph in Scripture), these two statements by Martha allude subtly to the story of Mary and Martha, sisters who seek to show their love for Christ by entertaining him in their home. Recorded in Luke 10:38-42, the story characterizes Mary as the embodiment of faith in and affection for Jesus and Martha as the practical worker:

> Now it came to pass, as they went, that he entered into a certain village: and a certain woman named Martha received him into her house.
> And she had a sister called Mary, which also sat at Jesus' feet, and heard his word.
> But Martha was cumbered about much serving, and came to him, and said, Lord, dost thou not care that my sister hath left me to serve alone? Bid her therefore that she help me.
> And Jesus answered and said unto her, Martha, Martha, thou art careful and troubled about many things:
> But one thing is needful: and Mary hath chosen that good part, which shall not be taken away from her.

Lena, too, has chosen well what governs her concerns. She is the embodiment of light and faith in others—the one who brings all other characters around her together, just as her travels help tie together the plot.

In addition to the numerous allusions to the Bible in *Light in August*, Faulkner may have in mind the Christian notion of time, in which people and events are either redeemed or destroyed. This sense of linear time is parodied in *Light in August*. Characters come to a minimal consciousness—if they awaken at all—and events are only momentarily illuminated. Faulkner's time is a cyclical journey, where some arbitrarily come into awareness, and others are denied even a glimpse of heaven. Christmas, claims Ursula Brumm, is "seized, tormented, and murdered, and in death he achieves an entirely unearthly transfiguration and something like spiritual resurrection."[33] To extend the parallels between Christ and Christmas this far is to ignore the horror of Christmas' death. No one cries, like the centurion at Christ's death, "Truly this man was the Son of God!" (Matt. 27:54). No curtain in the Temple is rent in two. Christmas dies alone, empty, his relatives crusading against him.

Here, too, is a parody, an ironic reflection of the Christ story. Faulkner's assertion that the "man seemed to rise soaring into their memories forever and ever" (440) follows Grimm's castration of Christmas. What the men will remember is the brutality; although Christmas, like Christ, is sacrificed, his violent death may be symbolic without being redemptive. Christmas does live and die, as Brumm appropriately notes, like other Faulkner heroes in their "grand doom."[34] But Christmas neither encounters nor provides salvation.

Before moving into a more thorough analysis of Hightower and Christmas, one must recognize that the Church, as in many of Faulkner's works, is not a neutral force. It has, Faulkner repeatedly implies, the power and the obligation to move into a needy world with balm and healing. Yet the Church in *Light in August* does not help Hightower or Christmas gain insight, and its passive rituals render it useless. Prayer and the Bible are not even mere panaceas, for Faulkner describes them as subversions of faith, as destructive forces. If Christmas is, as I have asserted, a symbol, then one cannot but listen to Hightower's words with dread: "Is it certain, proved, that he has negro blood? Think, Byron; what it will mean when the people—if they catch. . . . Poor man. Poor mankind" (93). It is Moseley who is cited earlier for his

---

[33]Ursula Brumm, *American Thought and Religious Typology* (New Brunswick NJ: Rutgers University Press, 1970) 207-208.

[34]Ursula Brumm, "The Figure of Christ in American Literature," *Partisan Review* 24 (1957): 413.

assertion that the Negro in us is the portion that knows how to endure, to prevail, through suffering. Just as the Christian community fails Christmas, the physical church itself proves ineffective. The frailty of the church, the hysterics of its supporters, and the light imagery developed throughout the novel converge in a key scene.

Fleeing his pursuers, Christmas runs into a Negro church, in which a service is in progress. The reader is told that Christmas "cursed God louder than the women screeching" (306). Then the church, the culture, and Christmas' own soul go dark.

> He [Christmas] stood there in the door, with the light behind him, laughing loud, and then he begun to curse again and we could see him snatch up a bench leg and swing it back. And we heard the first lamp bust, and it got dim in the church, and then we heard the other lamp bust and then it was dark and we couldn't see him no more (307).

It is a beleaguered Hightower who later sees the Church that has not served its purpose. In a passage that rings with anger, Hightower, the one-time preacher, gazes at the ruins of the Church. In this provocative section, one can see the divorce of the New Testament Christ and the modern church of the South:

> It seems to him that he has seen it all the while: that that which is destroying the Church is not the outward gropings of those within it nor the inward groping of those without, but the professionals who control it and who have removed the bells from its steeples. He seems to see them, endless, without order, empty, symbolical, bleak, skypointed not with ecstasy or passion but in adjuration, threat, and doom. He seems to see the churches of the world like a rampart, like one of those barricades of the middleages planted with dead and sharpened stakes, against truth and against that peace in which to sin and be forgiven which is the life of man (461).

The people who carry the hymnbooks to the church and worship will inevitably crucify Christmas. When Hightower flings himself before Grimm to rescue Christmas with a belated lie testifying to Christmas' whereabouts when Joanna is murdered, he is the true Church. Through this act, Hightower illustrates the humanness of a single man who needs justice meted out with mercy. In that instant, Christmas is not a symbol but a man. In that instant, Hightower rises above his townspeople who once "crossed the square [when] the church bells were ringing, slow and peaceful, and along the streets, the decorous people moved sedately beneath parasols, carrying Bibles and prayerbooks" (281). Christmas will be murdered because the decorous people cannot face the darkness in their own souls. Hightower prophesies to Bunch, "Since to pity him would be to admit self-doubt and to hope and need pity themselves. They will do it gladly, gladly. That's why it is so terrible, terrible, terrible" (348).

Hightower's marriage to the Church and his ostracism from it obsess Faulkner, who uses the life of the ex-minister as an allegory for the death of religion. "Denied by his church" (44), Hightower once pastored a Presbyterian congregation. When his wife dies mysteriously in Memphis after repeated absences from her hometown, Hightower "lost his church, he lost the Church" (53). Confusing his "heroic" dead grandfather with victory and religion, Hightower drives his followers away. Eventually, however, Hightower recognizes his grandfather as a thief killed while stealing chickens, sees himself as lost, and sees Christmas as an individual worth saving. He then becomes almost a mouthpiece for Faulkner, as he remembers Sunday evening prayer meeting: "Then alone, of all church gatherings, is there something of that peace which is the promise and the end of the Church" (346).

One has only to turn to McEachern's methods with a young Christmas to understand the horror of a Bible raised against another in rage or the destructive results of forced prayer. Here, as in Hightower's past, one sees religion misused. McEachern demands that the boy memorize his Presbyterian catechism; what lies next to his lesson book on the table is a less than enticing sight: "The boy sat in a straight chair beside the table on which was a nickel lamp and an enormous Bible with brass clasps and hinges and a brass lock" (137). With his voice later raised in fury at Christmas and his lover (calling her "Jezebel!" and "harlot!"), McEachern stands amidst the "sluttishness of weak human men" as the "actual representative of the wrathful and retributive Throne" (191). No merciful Christ is present in the man who systematically beats Christmas unconscious and who annihilates the love and forgiveness of the New Testament message. Forced into an attitude of prayer, Christmas never prays, remaining "calm, peaceful, quite inscrutable" (143) until he dies.

Thirty-three when he meets Joanna Burden, Christmas later kills her when she asks him to join her in prayer: "It's because she started praying over me. . . . That's it. Because she started praying over me . . . " (98). His life can be summarized by the scene in which a black caretaker confronts Christmas as a small boy. "I ain't a nigger," says the child, trying to integrate a name he has heard into his personality without knowing what the word means. The yard man responds, "You don't know what you are. And more than that, you won't never know. You'll live and you'll die and you won't never know. . . . don't nobody but God know what you is." And then, in a superb authorial intrusion, Faulkner writes, "But God wasn't there to say . . . " (363).

Prayer for Hightower, too, is initially like reading a drowsy Tennyson poem—and just as meaningful. Thinking "I should never have let myself get out of the habit of prayer," Hightower picks out a dog-eared volume by the Victorian poet:

> It does not take long. Soon the fine galloping language, the gutless swooning full of sapless trees and dehydrated lusts begins to swim smooth and swift and peaceful. It is better than praying without having to bother to think aloud. It is like listening in a cathedral to a eunuch chanting in a language which he does not even need to not understand (301).

Religion here lulls one into a half-life; it does not strengthen one for reality. Hightower eventually breaks out of the failed-Messiah pattern we have observed, wrenching out of linear Christian time and saving himself. During one dark night of the soul, Hightower helps to deliver a baby, Lena's child. After the child is born, Hightower goes home:

> And as he stands, tall, misshapen, lonely in his lonely and illkept kitchen, holding in his hand an iron skillet in which yesterday's old grease is bleakly caked, there goes through him a glow, a wave, a surge of something almost hot, almost triumphant. . . . He moves like a man with a purpose now, who for twentyfive years has been doing nothing at all between the time to wake and the time to sleep again. Neither is the book which he now chooses the Tennyson: this time also he chooses food for a man. It is Henry IV . . . (382-83).

It is the transformed minister of *Henry IV* who faces Grimm, his face bloodied, and cries, "Men! Listen to me. He was here that night. He was with me the night of the murder. I swear to God . . . " (439).

Beyond the allegorical implications of character, imagery, and allusions, *Light in August* ironically traces the life of Christ. As I have noted, Christmas' death is a distortion of the sacrifice of Christ, for Christmas dies, not to bring salvation, but to save the townspeople from having to look within themselves. One cannot divorce the quest of Christmas or Hightower from the light and dark imagery within the novel, for both are signals of the characters' inner struggles. Christmas cannot articulate his own search, so the reader must not expect the self-revelation of Faulkner's characters. Yet Faulkner is hardly subtle in his association of Christmas with darkness and the white race's night of guilt:

> The house was now *dark*, [Christmas] quit watching it then. He lay
> in the copse on his belly on the *dark* earth. In the copse the
> *darkness* was impenetrable. . . . His arms were crossed, his forehead
> rested upon them, in his nostrils the damp rich odor of the *dark*
> and fecund earth. . . . He did not look once again toward the *dark*
> house (215, italics mine).

Joanna Burden speaks of blacks "not as people, but as a thing, a shadow in which I lived, we lived, all white people, all other people" (239). Also, because Christmas can only attempt to define himself within the reference field of names and times, he is associated throughout *Light in August* with shadows. Here, too, he is juxtaposed with Christ, known in Scripture as the "Light of the World."

Christmas is described as shadow, a phantom, yet Faulkner's continued references to Christ and Joe remain disturbingly ironic. Through scattered allusions in the text (Mrs. McEachern's washing Joe's feet, the "slain sheep," a reference to Christmas' being thirty-three (213), and the description on page 332 of Joe's "bleeding sullen and quiet" at his trial), readers have no choice but to associate Joe with Christ. The moment they do, however, their categorization is undercut. "In the wide, empty, shadow-brooded street [Christmas] looked like a phantom, a spirit, strayed out of its own world, and lost" (106), writes Faulkner. Later, he describes Christmas as a child: "In the quiet and empty corridor, during the quiet hour of the early afternoon, he was like a shadow, small even for five years, sober and quiet as a shadow" (111). The shadowiness of his own self-perception traps and isolates him from the orphanage, to McEachern's house, to Joanna Burden's, to Hightower's. He can never assimilate or decipher the truth about himself, and he therefore becomes a pathetic rather than a tragic Christ-figure.

Faulkner toys with light and darkness as Christmas steps in and out of the "black hollow" (107) and "black pit" (108) of his origin, yet ultimately Christmas is swallowed up by the night. Fleeing from the townspeople, Christmas runs into the church described earlier, and he is pictured with the "light behind him" (306). The final tragedy of Christmas is not his brutal death but his inability to know himself. He is an ironic martyr, for he must pay in the human system for the murder of Joanna Burden; nonetheless, he is denied even a wrenching moment in Gethsemane in which to confess his fears or to justify his fate to himself. Christ died with forgiveness on his lips in an assurance of who he was, while Christmas crouches behind an overturned table, unsure even of why he had lived.

The fate of the Reverend Gail Hightower, on the other hand, is not pessimistic, although it is necessarily incomplete. Early in the novel, Hightower sits in his "poorly lighted" (44), stale home, waiting for oblivion. "The house, the study, is dark behind him, and he is waiting for that instant when all light has failed out of the sky" (55). Not only can he not unravel "religion and that galloping cavalry and his dead grandfather" (56), but his jumbled perception isolates and damns him. "I am not in life anymore," he tells Bunch. "That's why there is no use in even trying to meddle, interfere" (284). Yet by the end of his life, Hightower has meddled in both the birth of Lena's child and in Grimm's pursuit of Christmas. He also has assumed at least partial responsibility for the failure of his ministry and his marriage. Hightower's lessons are varied and episodic. He learns that the Church perverts and misunderstands its own hymns (347), that it denies the world the peace its founder promised (346), and that the professionals have killed its spirit (461).

Hightower says that because of his former obsession with his role in Jefferson, he must assume responsibility for his wife's fate: "I became her seducer, and her murderer, author and instrument of her shame and death" (462). Hightower also views the faces of his congregation and sees himself for the first time as a "charlatan preaching worse than heresy, in utter disregard of that whose very stage he preempted, offering instead of the crucified shape of pity and love, a swaggering and unchastened bravo killed with a shotgun in a peaceful henhouse, in a temporary hiatus of his own avocation of killing" (462). Religion and Hightower's grandfather resume their legitimate positions; the scales fall from their eyes.

In the course of the novel, Hightower learns pity ("Poor, barren woman [Joanna Burden]. To have not lived only a week longer, until luck returned to these barren and ruined acres" [in the shape of Lena's child]

—385). His renewed love for humanity, evidenced primarily in his concern for Byron Bunch, leads Hightower to an altered definition of himself. Awareness is dim but real, and Faulkner seems to believe that this must be enough. The "glow" (383) Hightower feels after delivering Lena's child is no accident, for Hightower's consciousness is coming awkwardly to life. Yet Hightower's long-awaited epiphany ends ambiguously. As the minister listens to the "dying thunder of hooves" (467), has he reverted to the darkness of fable? Is Faulkner saying that a man or woman may gain illumination for only a moment? Or does Hightower return to the scene of his failure only in order to see the parade of fantasy that has been his life? No definite answer emerges in the text, but the reader cannot afford to be too hopeful.

Faulkner follows closely on the heels of other American writers such as Katherine Anne Porter ("The Jilting of Granny Weatherall") and Emily Dickinson ("I heard a Fly buzz—when I died") in his awareness of humanity's sense of desertion in the face of death. Granny Weatherall feels jilted a second time when God fails to appear at her deathbed, while the speaker of Dickinson's poem expects a "King" and is greeted instead by a common insect. The reader is not even certain that Hightower has reached the end of his life. At the same time, Faulkner's highest tribute—delineated in his Nobel Prize speech—may be given Hightower. The individual, Faulkner states, "is immortal, not because he alone among creatures has an inexhaustible voice, but because he has a soul, a spirit capable of compassion and sacrifice and endurance."[35] Hightower has learned the greatest lesson of all; he has discovered his soul as he has responded to others. Nonetheless, Joe Christmas is dead.

Even in Faulkner's *Go Down, Moses,* the world waits in vain for a deliverer—neither the Old Testament Moses nor Gavin Stevens of the New South can really liberate his people. In *Light in August,* as well, no prophet steps forward to lead the nation. Hightower is ineffectual before Grimm, and he is not likely to save his community with his belated parcel of knowledge. Neither he nor Christmas has been dealt a fair hand by his fellows, and shadows remain in the "ruined garden" (264) of Faulkner's fictional world. In *The Wild Palms,* Faulkner writes, "If Jesus returned today we would have to crucify him quick in our own defense, to justify and preserve the civilization

---

[35]In *The Literature of the South,* eds., Thomas Daniel Young, Floyd C. Watkins, Richmond Croom Beatty (Chicago: Scott, Foresman, and Co., 1968) 1042.

we have worked and suffered and died shrieking and cursing in rage and impotence and terror for two thousand years to create and perfect in man's own image."[36] Beyond the promise offered through Hightower that humanity may look back and see its failures clearly, there is little hope in *Light in August*. There is a coming into consciousness, and an expensive awareness it is. But there is no Messiah.

---

[36]William Faulkner, *The Wild Palms* (New York: Random House, 1939) 136.

Conclusion

Honeysuckle. Martin Luther King, Jr. Kinfolks. Rosa Parks. Dixieland jazz. Jimmy Carter. The Confederacy. Jesse Helms. Hillbillies. George Wallace. The blues. Jesse Jackson. Rednecks. Billy Graham. The Bible Belt. Hank Aaron. Bluegrass. Elvis Presley. Mint julep. Huey Long. Grits and yokels.

References to the South in contemporary America abound, from Ken Burns' eleven-hour documentary "The Civil War" (PBS, 1990) to articles on Southern politicians in news magazines to television hits such as "Designing Women" and "Evening Shade." While those in American studies continue to question what George Lipsitz calls "the utility of national boundaries as fitting limits for the study of culture,"[1] *Allegory and the Modern Southern Novel* assumes a sympathy with such boundaries.

Regional studies provide a framework for the discussion of national character, although fragmentation is implicit in such an approach. In addition, studies of modern culture and literature allow an emphasis on the emerging images of the South often ignored in more established and restrictive analyses. Books such as *Media-Made Dixie: The South in the American Imagination* by Jack Temple Kirby (Athens: The University of Georgia Press, 1986) testify to the nation's continuing obsession with a region that defies easy categorization.

The role the South plays in America's understanding of its own culture has been—at best—an ambiguous one. The Deep South (Georgia, Alabama, Mississippi, Louisiana, and Florida) continues to struggle against poverty and ignorance, yet writers from these states have produced what modern literary critics acknowledge to be the second American Renascence (the first having occurred in New England from 1850–1855 with the work of Emily Dickinson, Walt Whitman, Nathaniel Hawthorne, Herman Melville, Ralph Waldo Emerson, Henry David Thoreau, and others). The influence of Hawthorne and Melville on the fiction of the modern South was examined in

---

[1]George Lipsitz, "Listening to Learn and Learning to Listen: Popular Culture, Cultural Theory, and American Studies," *American Quarterly* 42 (December 1990): 617.

chapter one: "The Evolution of Allegory in America." Much work remains to be done.

The second literary Renascence boasts William Faulkner, Tennessee Williams, Harper Lee, Carson McCullers, Flannery O'Connor, Eudora Welty, Katherine Anne Porter, Thomas Wolfe, Ralph Ellison, Robert Penn Warren, Truman Capote, Richard Wright, and others. Although the literary critics usually addicted to chronological groupings are alive and well, many hesitate to set inclusive years on this cultural explosion. The movement is far from finished.

In an article in *Newsweek*, reporter Gene Lyons quotes Walker Percy, who said in 1970, "The day of regional Southern writing is all gone. I think that people who try to write in that style are usually repeating a phased-out genre—or doing Faulkner badly."[2] While Percy's definition of "that style" is worth pursuing another time, Lyons goes immediately to the heart of the emergence of Southern novelists and scriptwriters important to this study. Responding to Percy's comment, Lyons writes,

> Well, maybe so. Could be all the stories worth telling have been told and the muse has picked up and left the Old Confederacy for good, leaving nothing behind but a mess of TV preachers peddling salvation to the sleek suburbanites of "the New South"—a region now indistinguishable from the suburbs of Cleveland. If so, somebody needs to get the word to Southern fiction writers, not to mention the publishers, booksellers, and readers of the region. They're acting as if they hadn't heard.[3]

Included in the most recent wave of Southern writers are Bobbie Ann Mason, Anne Tyler, Shirley Ann Grau, Walker Percy, T. R. Pearson, Peter Taylor, Ellen Gilchrist, Gail Goodwin, William Styron, Alice Walker, Robert Penn Warren (who bridges the old and new, as does Eudora Welty) and others.

Curiosity about the region draped in mystery and moonlight never ebbs, but the South continues to be characterized in much the same way as it was in the early 1900s. Recognizing on one level that sexism and racism are pervasive national crimes and that anti-intellectualism exists across the United

---

[2]Quoted by Gene Lyons, "The South Rises Again: a new generation of writers has emerged in Dixie," *Newsweek* (30 September 1985) 71.
[3]Ibid.

States, critics, writers, politicians, and educators still point to the South as representative of these cultural evils. This characterization both deflects the guilt the rest of the country shares with its Southern neighbors and becomes a part of the national fabric as reflected in contemporary literature, film, and television programming.

However, the South has itself absorbed much of the national perception and has thereby become more self-reflective and introspective. The emergence of allegorical literature in the region is no accident, for Southern writers have continually sought a medium to communicate the universality of their themes: (1) the existence of evil within the individual, (2) the repercussions of guilt and revenge, and (3) the desire of humankind for happiness and secular/religious salvation from failure and sin.

The conclusions about the nature of the South relayed in contemporary literature may be summarized as follows:

> (1) The South is a distinct region peopled by grotesques who may appear foolish but who secretly safeguard the highest human values.

> (2) The South is a distinct region endowed with a philosophical and religious perspective that makes it more cognizant of the implications of original sin and human failure than the rest of the nation. After its sound defeat in the Civil War, the South understands the perils of America's sacrificing itself in a potential lost cause.

> (3) The South is a distinct region that relies on a rural economy and a belief in the value of the land and the importance of family.

These claims remain for other writers to explore; their importance in *Allegory and the Modern Southern Novel* lies in their having been readily assimilated into the national consciousness and their clear connection with the necessity for allegorical reenactment in the fiction of the South.

Jonathan W. Daniels (1902–1981), former editor of the *Raleigh (N.C.) News and Observer,* writes, "We Southerners are a mythological people, created half out of dreams and half out of slander, who live in a still legendary land."[4] This legendary land is the sum and substance of allegory, a realm in which characters can play out the war between good and evil and can seek self-awareness and remain representative of humankind.

The South stands as a reminder of one of the worst crimes ever committed against humanity, as a symbol of human greed and selfishness. The depiction of slavery and the murder of a man who fears he is part black in *Go Down, Moses* and *Light in August*, respectively, leave no defense for the blight on the history of the South. The search for a savior in *The Heart Is a Lonely Hunter* by Carson McCullers and in *Wise Blood* by Flannery O'Connor indicates the longing of the Southern writer to understand the crimes we commit against each other and the desire for a savior and for absolution.

But the South stands, also, as a reminder of brighter days, days of porch swings, spelling bees, fireflies and honeysuckle, days of dusty roads and church socials and picnic blankets beside quiet streams. The allegories of the South explored in this study recreate a land of natural beauty and a deep commitment to religion and personal faith; they point to an American investment in the values of rural, small-town life and the human need for community. If Flannery O'Connor is correct, grace often comes through violence and despair, and the South as a region has experienced both.

Our national nostalgia for the land of magnolias and roadside stands is based, perhaps, on a longing for days and times we only imagine we knew.

---

[4]Quoted by George B. Tindall in *Encyclopedia of Southern Culture*, eds., Charles Reagan Wilson and William Ferris (Chapel Hill NC: University of North Carolina Press, 1989) 1097.

Bibliography

Abrams, M. H., ed. *The Norton Anthology of English Literature*, Vol. 1. New York: W. W. Norton, 1968.

Ackermann, R. D. "The Immolation of Isaac McCaslin." *Texas Studies in Language and Literature* 16 (Fall 1974): 564.

Adamowski, T. H. "Isaac McCaslin and the Wilderness of the Imagination." *The Centennial Review* 17 (Winter 1973): 92-112.

Auerbach, Erich. *Scenes from the Drama of European Literature*. New York: Meridian Books, 1959.

Barth, J. Robert. *The Symbolic Imagination: Coleridge and the Romantic Tradition*. Princeton NJ: Princeton University Press, 1977.

Becker, John E. *Hawthorne's Historical Allegory: An Examination of the American Conscience*. New York: Kennikat Press, 1971.

Bercovitch, Sacvan. *The American Jeremiad*. Madison WI: University of Wisconsin Press, 1978.

_____. *The American Puritan Imagination*. New York: Cambridge University Press, 1974.

_____. *Typology and Early American Literature*. Amherst MA: University of Massachusetts, 1972.

Bloom, Edward A. "The Allegorical Principle." *Journal of English Literary History* 18 (September 1951): 163-90.

Bornkamm, Günther. *Jesus of Nazareth*. New York: Harper and Row, 1960.

Brumm, Ursula. *American Thought and Religious Typology*. New Brunswick NJ: Rutgers University Press, 1970.

_____. "The Figure of Christ in American Literature." *Partisan Review* 24 (1957): 403-13.

Burns, Stuart L. "The Evolution of *Wise Blood.*" *Modern Fiction Studies* 16 (Summer 1970): 147-62.

_____. "Freaks in a Circus Tent: Flannery O'Connor's Christ-Haunted Characters." *The Flannery O'Connor Bulletin* 1 (Autumn 1972): 3-23.

Carr, Virginia Spencer. *The Lonely Hunter*. New York: Doubleday and Company, 1975.

Cash, W. J. *The Mind of the South*. New York: Doubleday and Company, 1954.

Cassill, R. V., ed. *The Norton Anthology of Short Fiction*. New York: W. W. Norton and Co., 1978.

Chase, Richard. *The American Novel and Its Tradition*. Baltimore: Johns Hopkins University Press, 1957.

Clifford, Gay. *The Transformations of Allegory*. Boston: Routledge and Kegan Paul, 1974.

Coleridge, Samuel Taylor. *The Collected Works of Samuel Taylor Coleridge*. Edited by R. J. White. Princeton NJ: Princeton University Press, 1972.

Cook, Richard M. *Carson McCullers*. New York: Frederick Ungar Publishing Co., 1975.

Cowain, Bainard. *Exiled Waters: Moby-Dick and the Crisis of Allegory*. Baton Rouge LA: Louisiana State University Press, 1982.

Cowley, Malcolm. "Go Down to Faulkner's Land." *The New Republic* 106 (29 June 1942).

Daniels, Jonathan W. Quoted by George B. Tindall in "Mythic South." *Encyclopedia of Southern Culture.* Edited by Charles Reagan Wilson and William Ferris. Chapel Hill NC: University of North Carolina Press, 1989.

De Man, Paul. *Allegories of Reading: Figural Language in Rousseau, Nietzsche Rilke, and Proust.* New Haven: Yale University Press, 1979.

Detweiler, Robert. "Christ and the Christ Figure in American Fiction." *The Christian Scholar* 47 (1964): 111-24.

Devlin, Albert J. " 'How Much It Takes to Compound a Man': A Neglected Scene in *Go Down, Moses.*" *The Midwest Quarterly* 14 (Summer 1973): 408-21.

Dillenberger, John, ed. *John Calvin: Selections from His Writings.* New York: Doubleday and Company, 1971.

Dillistone, F. W. *The Novelist and the Passion Story.* New York: Sheed and Ward, 1960.

Doubleday, Neal Frank. *Hawthorne's Early Tales.* Durham NC: Duke University Press, 1972.

Early, James. *Making of Go Down, Moses.* Dallas TX: Southern Methodist University Press, 1972.

Emerson, Everett. *Puritanism in America.* Boston: Twayne Publishers, 1977.

Emerson, Ralph Waldo. *Selected Prose and Poetry.* Edited by Reginald L. Cook. New York: Holt, Rinehart, and Winston, 1969.

Fant, Joseph L., and Robert Ashley. *Faulkner at West Point.* New York: Random House, 1964.

Faulkner, William. "The Art of Fiction," by Jean Stein. *Paris Review* 12 (Spring 1956): 28-52.

_____. *A Fable.* New York: Random House, 1950.

_____. *Go Down, Moses.* New York: Random House, 1942.

_____. *Light in August.* New York: Random House, 1932.

_____. "Nobel Prize Speech." In *The Literature of the South.* Ed. Thomas Daniel Young and Floyd C. Watkins. Chicago: Scott Foresman and Co., 1968.

_____. *The Sound and the Fury.* New York: Random House, 1929.

_____. *The Wild Palms.* New York: Random House, 1939.

Feidelson, Charles. *Symbolism and American Literature.* Chicago: University of Chicago Press, 1953.

Fletcher, Angus. *Allegory: The Theory of a Symbolic Mode.* Ithaca NY: Cornell University Press, 1964.

Fogle, Richard Harter. *Hawthorne's Fiction: The Light and the Dark.* Norman OK: University of Oklahoma Press, 1952.

Foster, Elizabeth S. *The Confidence-Man: His Masquerade,* by Herman Melville. Introduction. New York: Hendricks House, 1954.

Friedman, Melvin J., ed. *The Added Dimension.* New York: Fordham University Press, 1977.

Frost, Robert. "Directive." In *The Poetry of Robert Frost.* Edited by Edward C. Lathem. New York: Holt, Rinehart, and Winston, 1969.

Frye, Northrop. *Anatomy of Criticism.* Princeton NJ: Princeton University Press, 1957.

Harter, Carol Clancey. "The Winter of Isaac McCaslin: Revisions and Irony in Faulkner's 'Delta Autumn.' " *Journal of Modern Literature* 1 (1970): 209-25.

Harvard, William C., and Walter Sullivan, eds. *A Band of Prophets: The Vanderbilt Agrarians after Fifty Years.* Baton Rouge LA: Louisiana State University Press, 1982.

Hawthorne, Nathaniel. *The English Notebooks.* Edited by Randall Stewart. New York: Russell and Russell, Inc., 1969.

_____. *Great Short Works of Hawthorne.* Edited by Frederick C. Crews. New York: Harper and Row, 1967.

_____. *The Portable Hawthorne.* Edited by Malcolm Cowley. New York: Viking Press, 1969.

Herbert, T. Walter. *Moby-Dick and Calvinism: A World Dismantled.* Brunswick NJ: Rutgers University Press, 1977.

Honig, Edwin. *Dark Conceit: The Making of Allegory.* Evanston IL: Northwestern University Press, 1959.

Ibsen, Henrik. *Brand.* New York: Doubleday and Company, 1960. *I'll Take My Stand: The South and the Agrarian Tradition.* New York: Harper and Brothers, 1930.

Kafka, Franz. *The Complete Stories and Parables.* New York: Book of the Month Club, 1983.

Kierkegaard, Søren. *Attack upon Christendom.* Translated by Walter Lowrie. Princeton NJ: Princeton University Press, 1944.

_____. *Parables of Kierkegaard.* Edited by Thomas C. Oden. Princeton NJ: Princeton University Press, 1978.

Lawrence, D. H., *St. Mawr and the Man Who Died.* New York: Random House, 1953.

Leary, Lewis. *Southern Excursions.* Baton Rouge LA: Louisiana State University Press, 1971.

Lee, Harper. *To Kill A Mockingbird.* New York: J. B. Lippincott and Co., 1960.

Lewis, C. S. *The Allegory of Love: A Study in Medieval Tradition.* London: Oxford University Press, 1938.

Lipsitz, George. "Listening to Learn and Learning to Listen: Popular Culture, Cultural Theory, and American Studies." *American Quarterly* 42 (December 1990): 615-36.

Littlefield, Daniel F. "Flannery O'Connor's *Wise Blood:* 'Unparalleled Prosperity' and Spiritual Chaos." *Mississippi Quarterly* 23 (Spring 1970): 121-33.

Long, Robert Emmet. *The Great Succession: Henry James and the Legacy of Hawthorne.* Pittsburgh: University of Pittsburgh Press, 1979.

Lyons, Gene. "The South Rises Again: A new generation of writers has emerged in Dixie." *Newsweek* (30 September 1985): 71, 73-74.

MacNeice, Louis. *Varieties of Parable.* Cambridge: Cambridge University Press, 1965.

May, John R. *The Pruning Word: The Parables of Flannery O'Connor.* Notre Dame ID: University of Notre Dame Press, 1976.

McCullers, Carson. *The Heart Is a Lonely Hunter.* New York: Houghton Mifflin Co., 1977.

_____. *The Mortgaged Heart.* Edited by Margarita G. Smith. Boston: Houghton Mifflin Co., 1971.

McDowell, Margaret B. *Carson McCullers.* Boston: Twayne Publishers, 1980.

McGiffert, Michael. *Puritanism and the American Experience.* Reading MA: Addison-Wesley, 1969.

McMichael, George, ed. *Anthology of American Literature.* 2d ed. New York: Macmillan Publishing Co., 1980.

McNeill, John T. *The History and Character of Calvinism.* New York: Oxford University Press, 1954.

Melville, Herman. *The Confidence-Man.* Afterword by R. W. B. Lewis. New York: New American Library, 1964.

_____. *The Letters of Herman Melville.* Edited by Merrell R. Davis and William H. Gilman. New Haven: Yale University Press, 1960.

_____. *Romances of Herman Melville.* New York: Tudor Publishing, 1931.

Meriwether, James, and Michael Millgate. *Lion in the Garden: Interviews with William Faulkner.* New York: Random House, 1968.

Milder, Robert. "The Protestantism of Flannery O'Connor." *The Southern Review* 11 (1975): 802-19.

Miller, Perry, ed. *The American Transcendentalists.* Baltimore: Johns Hopkins University Press, 1957.

_____. *The Puritans.* 2 vols. New York: Harper and Row, 1963.

Millgate, Michael. *The Achievement of William Faulkner.* New York: Random House, 1966.

_____. *Faulkner.* New York: Capricorn Books, 1971.

Moseley, Edwin. *Pseudonyms of Christ in the Modern Novel.* Pittsburgh: University of Pittsburgh Press, 1962.

Muller, Gilbert H. *Nightmares and Visions: Flannery O'Connor and the Catholic Grotesque.* Athens GA: University of Georgia Press, 1972.

Niebuhr, Reinhold. *The Irony of American History.* New York: Charles Scribner's Sons, 1952.

Nietzsche, Friedrich. *The Gay Science.* In *Existentialism from Dostoevsky to Sartre.* New York: New American Library, 1975.

O'Connor, Flannery. *The Complete Stories.* New York: Farrar, Straus, & Giroux, 1973.

_____. *The Habit of Being.* Edited by Sally Fitzgerald. New York: Farrar, Straus & Giroux, 1973.

_____. *Mystery and Manners.* Edited by Sally and Robert Fitzgerald. New York: Farrar, Straus, & Giroux, 1969.

_____. *Wise Blood.* New York: New American Library, 1962.

Orvell, Miles. *Invisible Parade.* Philadelphia: Temple University Press, 1972.

Percy, Walker. *Love in the Ruins: The Adventures of a Bad Catholic at a Time Near the End of the World.* New York: Farrar, Straus, & Giroux, 1971.

_____. *The Second Coming.* New York: Farrar, Straus, & Giroux, 1980.

Presley, Delma Eugene. "Carson McCullers and the South." *The Georgia Review* 28 (Spring 1974): 19-32.

Quilligan, Maureen. *The Language of Allegory.* Ithaca NY: Cornell University Press, 1979.

Richardson, Robert D. *Myth and Literature in the American Renaissance.* Bloomington IN: Indiana University Press, 1978.

Rilke, Rainer Maria. *Duino Elegies and the Sonnets to Orpheus.* Translated by A. Poulin, Jr. Boston: Houghton Mifflin, 1977.

Rubin, Louis D., ed. *Southern Literary Study: Problems and Possibilities.* Chapel Hill NC: University of North Carolina Press, 1975.

Rutman, Darrett. *American Puritanism.* New York: J. B. Lippincott, 1970.

Shakespeare, William. *Hamlet.* In *William Shakespeare: The Complete Works.* Edited by Alfred Harbage. Baltimore: Penguin Books, 1969.

Shloss, Carol. *Flannery O'Connor's Dark Comedies.* Baton Rouge LA: Louisiana State University Press, 1980.

Singal, Daniel Joseph. *The War Within (From Victorian to Modernist Thought in the South, 1919–45).* Chapel Hill NC: University of North Carolina Press, 1982.

Steele, David N., and Curtis C. Thomas. *The Five Points of Calvinism.* Philadelphia: Presbyterian and Reformed Publishing Co., 1965.

Sullivan, Walter. *Death by Melancholy: Essays on Modern Southern Fiction.* Baton Rouge LA: Louisiana State University Press, 1972.

TeSelle, Sallie. *Speaking in Parables: A Study in Metaphor and Theology.* Philadelphia: Fortress Press, 1975.

Thompson, Lawrance. *Melville's Quarrel with God.* Princeton NJ: Princeton University Press, 1952.

Thoreau, Henry David. *The Portable Thoreau.* Edited by Carl Bode. New York: Penguin Books, 1947.

Toynbee, Arnold J. *A Study of History: Vol. I–VI.* Edited by D. C. Somervell. New York: Oxford University Press, 1947.

Turner, Arlin. *Nathaniel Hawthorne.* New York: Barnes and Noble, 1961.

Vaughan, Alden T., and Francis J. Bremer, eds. *Puritan New England.* New York: St. Martin's Press, 1977.

Warren, Robert Penn. *All the King's Men.* New York: Bantam Books, 1946.

Widmer, Kingsley. *The Ways of Nihilism: A Study of Herman Melville's Short Novels.* Los Angeles: California State Colleges, 1970.

Wilson, Edmund, ed. *The Shock of Recognition.* New York: Farrar, Straus, and Cudahy, 1943.

Woodward, C. Vann. *The Burden of Southern History.* Baton Rouge LA: Louisiana State University Press, 1960.

Ziolkowski, Theodore. *Fictional Transfigurations of Jesus.* Princeton NJ: Princeton University Press, 1972.

Index